"Few mysteries confound business leaders more than how creative professionals work their magic. In *Strategic Creativity*, Robin Landa pulls back the veil to reveal the hidden logic of great marketing communications, from copywriting to graphic design to brand design. Armed with the insights in this book, business leaders will have a vastly easier time interfacing with creative professionals to produce game-changing marketing communications. Filled with compelling insights, checklists, and real-world business cases, *Strategic Creativity* drills into the details yet never loses sight of the big strategic picture: to build brands with purpose and humanity."

Neal Roese, *Professor and Chair of the Marketing Department, Kellogg School of Management, Northwestern University*

"Robin Landa has written a fascinating new book on *Strategic Creativity*. The book hands executives the keys to harnessing the best out of creative professionals while also learning how to generate ideas and be more creative yourself. This guided tour of strategic creativity should be on the desk of anyone hoping to build a strong brand, fine tune your advertising, and avoid costly mistakes."

Paul A. Argenti, *Professor of Corporate Communication, The Tuck School of Business at Dartmouth*

"Professor Landa has written a remarkable and valuable book, simultaneously enlightening and pragmatic. Business professionals are the customers of advertising, but rarely understand or contribute to what they are 'buying.' This book enables a business professional to rise above their peers with superior creative outcomes as well as enhances their ability to communicate the 'why' throughout their organization. Landa provides a compelling rationale and checklists in a stepwise manner and illustrates them with clear examples. If only I had read this at the start of my career!"

Donald Fishbein, *Senior Biotech and Pharmaceutical Executive*

"Again and again, Robin Landa has brought forth her inexhaustible well of creativity to help us see and deal with the world in new and imaginative ways. Now with her latest work, *Strategic Creativity*, she shows us how to use our own imaginative understanding in a detailed way that guides us to achieving our overall aims and intentions in a variety of environments. This highly original volume provides a practical handbook to harnessing the creative potential within us all."

Professor Craig P. Donovan, *Kean University Senate Chair*

"Robin Landa has done it again! This is a must-read for anyone in the marketing or advertising industry who wants to be the one business person in the room who speaks knowledgeably about creative directions and solutions. This explains the importance of strategic creativity better than I ever could."

Brooke Roderick, *Senior Art Director, VCCP*

"Marketers, strategists, and business owners alike will benefit from reading Robin Landa's book, *Strategic Creativity*. This book is filled with important and easily digestible advice that you won't find anywhere on 'Dr. Internet.' It's apparent that a significant amount of research has gone into this book, and as a marketing strategist and business owner myself, I plan to revisit *Strategic Creativity* again and again. Robin defines exactly what brands need to do to make consumers stop their scrolling and take notice. As Robin mentions, the riskiest idea is the one people will *not* notice. If you don't take notice of this book, you are missing out on an incredibly valuable read."

Megan Lynn Levy, *Entrepreneur and Marketer*

"*Strategic Creativity* is one of those books that no matter where you open it, you'll find creative insights that you can use in your everyday. I found myself making notes throughout the entire read. Robin's writing and way of storytelling are engaging and easy to follow. It all just makes sense and will have you asking yourself, as well as others, all the right questions. It's an ace in your back pocket when dealing with creative teams. *Strategic Creativity* will have you zeroing in on the 'WHY' and should be in every exec's toolbox."

Mike Sickinger, *Art Director*

"Robin Landa's new book distills the complexity out of modern marketing decision-making. You'll be more strategic, more creative, and more effective after reading this great playbook."

Drew Neisser, *Founder, Renegade & CMO Huddles and Author of* Renegade Marketing: 12 Steps to Building Unbeatable B2B Brands

"*Strategic Creativity* is essential for any brand, particularly creating a compelling story about a brand, product, or service that stands out from the noise and sticks with the intended audience. When done well, buyers feel a connection to the brand and the message resonates. This book provides a solid framework to help organizations think beyond the status quo, which is a trap many brands fall into today. Landa packs a lot of valuable information into every chapter."

Lauri A. Harrison, *Lecturer, Business Certificate Program, Columbia University, School of Professional Studies*

Strategic Creativity

The secret weapon for business experts to ensure strategically creative results, this is an indispensable field guide to evaluating creative advertising, branding, and design ideas and solutions, and to working with creatives.

Strategic Creativity is a fundamental resource that enables business professionals to stand out amongst their colleagues and enhance their ability to communicate the creative "why" throughout their organizations, and it covers what every business expert should fully comprehend about the creative process. To effectively grow a business and reach the right audience or move a brand forward, advertising and branding need to be relevant, engaging, and worth people's time. This book contains what a CEO, CMO, manager, business owner, or client didn't learn about the creative side of advertising and design in business school.

Featuring insightful conversations with creative experts, this book will earn a place on the desks of executives, leaders, managers, and middle managers across industries, whose work requires them to understand and execute on branding initiatives, advertising campaigns, social media, and other customer-facing content.

Robin Landa is an expert in creative advertising, branding, graphic design, and social media, and has been called a "creativity guru," having published over 20 widely recognized books in her fields of expertise. Robin holds the title of Distinguished Professor of the Michael Graves College, Kean University, USA. She has won numerous awards for her design, writing, and research, and the Carnegie Foundation lists her among the greatest teachers of our time. Robin is a former chair of Design Incubation and serves as a creative consultant to the C-suites of international corporations. You can find out more about her work online at Robinlanda.com

Strategic Creativity

A Business Field Guide to Advertising, Branding, and Design

Robin Landa

Routledge
Taylor & Francis Group

NEW YORK AND LONDON

Cover design and chapter openers: Romit Sarkar

First published 2022
by Routledge
605 Third Avenue, New York, NY 10158

and by Routledge
4 Park Square, Milton Park, Abingdon, Oxon, OX14 4RN

Routledge is an imprint of the Taylor & Francis Group, an informa business

Library of Congress Cataloging-in-Publication Data
Names: Landa, Robin, author.
Title: Strategic creativity: a business field guide to advertising,
branding, and design / Robin Landa.
Description: New York, NY: Routledge, 2022. | Includes bibliographical
references and index. |
Identifiers: LCCN 2021057002 | ISBN 9781032137803 (hardback) | ISBN
9781032137797 (paperback) | ISBN 9781003230786 (ebook)
Subjects: LCSH: Creative ability in business. | Commercial art. | Branding
(Marketing) | Advertising. | Communication in marketing.
Classification: LCC HD53 .L363 2022 | DDC 650.1--dc23/eng/20220126
LC record available at https://lccn.loc.gov/2021057002

ISBN: 978-1-032-13780-3 (hbk)
ISBN: 978-1-032-13779-7 (pbk)
ISBN: 978-1-003-23078-6 (ebk)

DOI: 10.4324/9781003230786

Typeset in Freight
by Deanta Global Publishing Services, Chennai, India

For everyone who could use a secret superpower.

Contents

Foreword

Deborah Ceballos

Creative Director/Partner, Square Melon Communications

There I was, telling my personal trainer how I was eager to work on my abs—intensely focused on my midsection and ready to commit to hundreds of crunches. My trainer simply shook his head and advised, "You'll hurt yourself if you only attack your core without first striving for overall strength and balance!"

Although you did not pick up this book to learn the secret to core strength, you will discover many secrets to succeeding in business. Once you finish this book, all your intentions and efforts, once integrated, will lead to thriving business practices.

Figure 0.1 Deborah Ceballos

If you are a business owner, CEO, CMO, marketing manager, or any other type of business or marketing professional, the wisdom in *Strategic Creativity* will help you achieve that overall strength and balance that your marketing approach requires. You will achieve the results that will help you stand apart from your peers with a solid core that radiates through the rest of your business.

Creative practitioners have sat at the table for decades now. To work more effectively with them, start by understanding their process and demonstrating your knowledge to everyone on the team and in your company. *Strategic Creativity* reinvents what a business or marketing education should encompass to get results.

Consider *Strategic Creativity* your personal trainer in dealing with creative practitioners, collaborating with creatives, evaluating creative solutions, and killing any pedestrian ideas before those "meh" ideas dispatch the brand or your career. As Donald Fishbein, senior biotech and pharmaceutical executive, said after reading it, "If only I had read this at the start of my career!"

If you're someone who wants a handle on what makes advertising, branding, and design tick and resonate, this book is for you. Much like circuit training, it breaks down the creative process into approachable sets that target what constitutes strategically creative advertising, branding, and design solutions.

As a past president of the Art Directors Club of New Jersey, a current professor of advertising, and a founder of my own agency, running it for the past 17 years, I understand the power this book holds in bridging the creative and the business arms of our industries. Landa's mentorship from the start of my career has directly influenced the success of my business and the importance of continued communication between terrific CEOs, CMOs, clients, and marketing managers, and really savvy business professionals. If only they had read Landa's book, our conversations would have been effortless.

Strategic Creativity taps into what makes work great. Compelling best-practice information, persuasive quotes, interviews with esteemed creative professionals, such as Rei Inamoto, Lisa Smith, and Nick Sonderup, as well as prominent experts in psychology, make this book unprecedented.

By truly understanding the creative side, you are in a position of greater power. *Strategic Creativity*, at its core, explicitly establishes how the practice of strategic creativity in advertising, branding, and design depends upon intentional and inspired ideas that people will find relevant and resonating. In addition, it stands to be a primer on design, brand storytelling, copywriting, art direction, and more, unlike any other business book.

You are holding a secret weapon, as Landa says. Her contribution to the disciplines of advertising, branding, and graphic design is unmatched. Robin Landa has written 23 books on these subjects, is a consultant to major companies and marketing directors, and holds the title of Distinguished Professor in the Michael Graves College of Kean University. At its core, this book offers you the knowledge that will transform you into the most creatively savvy business person in the room.

Acknowledgements

A huge thank you to all the brilliant people who contributed to my research and this book: Rachel Abrams, Olu Adewalure, Jason Alejandro, Gail Anderson, Dr. Paul A. Argenti, Dr. Jill Bellinson, Greg Braun, Steven Brower, Leigh Muzslay Browne, Nancy Campbell, Deborah Ceballos, Emily Jing Sum Chan, Ross Chowles, Ana Paola Noriega Cid, Alexandre Collares, Brian Collins, Rick Cosgrove, Jennifer Chang Coupland, Natalia Delgado, Liz DeLuna, Dr. Craig Donovan, Alice Drueding, Omar Emera, Erin Evon, Dr. Fred M. Feinberg, Mike Felix, Donald Fishbein, Danielle Garcia, Christine Gratton, Natalie Greenman, Dr. Elizabeth Guffey, Lauri A. Harrison, Jamie Kecnan, Thomas Kemeny, Paul Kemp-Robertson, Dr. Ajay K. Kohli, Rei Inamoto, Alexander Isley, Scott Laserow, Lou Leonardis, Kristin Leu, Megan Lynn Levy, Dr. Donald R. Marks, Amy Maw, Trevett McCandliss, Jose Molla, Justin Moore, Chris Navetta, Drew Neisser, Dr. Bob Nelson, Mariana Peluffo, Alison Place, Rob Reilly, NiRey Reynolds, Brooke Roderick, Dr. Neal Roese, Julia Ross, Joe Scorsone, Camille Sherrod, Mike Sickinger, Lisa Smith, Mariana Sokolowski, Nick Sonderup, Henry Stankiewicz, Jackie Sumsky, Nijel Taylor, Danielle Thomas, Aggie Toppins, Rich Tu, Jennifer Vandersteen, and Jessica Walsh.

For their abundant support, my thanks to the Kean University administration: Dr. Lamont Repollet, President; Dr. David S. Birdsell, Provost and Senior Vice President; Dr. Jeffrey Toney, Senior Vice President for Research; Dr. Joy Moskovitz, Assistant Provost and Vice President; David Mohney, Dean of the Michael Graves College; Rose Gonnella, Associate Design of the Michael Graves College; Reenat Hasan Munshi, Managing Director of the Office of Research and Sponsored Programs; and the Release Time for Research & Creative Works Committee. Thank you to my colleagues for their support of my release time proposal. My thanks to Terry Clague and Louise Baird-Smith for their generosity and referrals.

My great thanks to Meredith Norwich, Senior Editor, Routledge/Taylor & Francis, for her terrific support, insights, and graciousness. My thanks to Chloe Herbert, editorial assistant, Routledge/Taylor & Francis. I am grateful to Ann M. Hale for her excellent copy editing, advice, and patience. I would like to express my appreciation to Abigail Stanley and Stacey Carter at Taylor & Francis UK for their help with this publication and for their great collegiality.

Huge thanks to Romit Sarkar for his outstanding cover design, chapter openers, and diagrams, and to Mara Reyes for her splendid diagrammatic illustrations.

Finally, thanks to Dr. Harry Gruenspan and Hayley Gruenspan for their unreserved encouragement of my work. I just wish I could beat them in a game of *Jeopardy*.

To all and for all, I am grateful.

Preface

Strategic Creativity is the story of a secret superpower.

The person who possesses Strategic Creativity is tactical, resourceful, ingenious, cunning, and extremely attractive (perhaps I'm getting carried away). An infiltrator, influencer, and eavesdropper. If you possess Strategic Creativity, you know what will call people to action, what will make them feel special and heard, what will entertain them or change their thinking. And you will be the business professional with super skills every designer respects.

Fine artists have the luxury of being creative—they're not communicating with mass audiences. Not so for creative directors, art directors, copywriters, brand designers, and graphic designers; their creative thinking must be tactical—they must possess this secret power. Strategic creativity provides these folks with a handle on what people desire or need—even before people know they want it or need it.

For you—sitting in the C-suite, a leader, a business owner, or a business professional involved in advertising, branding, and design—to get what you need to launch a brand, entity, or individual, to move a brand forward, to grow a business, or to raise funds, you need us—secret agents who conceive and construct strategic creative solutions. And yours truly is willing to share her know-how.

With the insights into the creative process found here, you'll be the business pro the creative team will respect most and listen to—which would set you apart from your peers.

You also need to *know what will work and why* it's well conceived, well designed, well written, or art directed. And why pedestrian ideas won't get you anywhere except the unemployment line.

You'll find illuminating interviews with industry leaders, agency heads, psychologists, AIGA Gold Medalists, as well as a creative professional who is a few years into his career.

Think of me as your personal "Alfred Pennyworth"—I'm your special creative forces wingman, who will be supplying all you need to commission and evaluate creative solutions and to cooperate and collaborate with creative professionals.

My hope for you, dear reader, is this book will be your strategic advantage, equipping you with a secret superpower—Strategic Creativity. Please feel free to invent your own code name.

Carry on.

Yours,
Landa. Robin Landa.

One of the guiding maxims at I&CO is—
'Risk nothing, change nothing.'

—Rei Inamoto

Chapter 1

Why Strategic Creativity

The Value of Strategic Creativity

If you've ever consulted "Dr. Internet" about a medical issue, then this cautionary tale is for you. Furthermore, if you are not a graphic designer and have designed your own logo, please don't tell me because I want to keep this read friendly.

Lots of folks in Romania may have an overconfidence bias, which psychologist Daniel Kahneman calls the "most significant of the cognitive biases." According to *Vice* magazine journalist Mihai Popescu, three-quarters of people in Romania take medication without consulting doctors. To encourage people in Romania to seek medical attention, McCann Bucharest partnered with *Vice* for Regina Maria, one of the biggest healthcare providers in Romania. They introduced the "Internet's Residency Exam" to put "Dr. Internet" to the test. Held on the same day as the national official residency exam for doctors, *Vice* journalist Popescu, along with hundreds of real doctors, took the exam with only access to the Internet. Popescu had to answer 200 questions in four hours. His score? 36 correct out of 200.

Then the Regina Maria ad campaign opened the challenge to everyone with an online tool. When people failed the exam, they received a voucher they could use at Regina Maria clinics. McCann says, they even hijacked Google "by targeting the most common symptom searches in Romania and encouraging people to visit a real doctor," while the media turned their campaign into a public interest story.

Greta Redeleanu, marketing director of Regina Maria, told *Little Black Book*:

> As leader in the quality of medical services, we have a responsibility towards patients, and we believe it's our duty to invest in educational and prevention campaigns. Even if we are not doctors, but marketing professionals, we understand the responsibility we all have: not just to do good, but to develop relevant campaigns and initiatives to change mentalities, to raise awareness regarding the importance of going to the doctor for periodical health checks and screenings, appropriate for every age category.[1]

I'm sure you don't want the graphic design, branding, or ad campaigns you commission to score a 36 out of 200.

That's why I wrote *Strategic Creativity*, to help you better understand the creative side of advertising, branding, and graphic design well enough so you

DOI: 10.4324/9781003230786-1

can commission, evaluate, collaborate, and effectively interact with creative professionals, contribute to the creative process in a meaningful way, and get effective solutions to drive the results you, your company, or your clients need. *After you read this book, you'll be the only business professional in the room who can explain the origin and meaning of your agency's campaign, which will set you apart and above your peers!*

"Business professionals are the customers of advertising, but rarely understand or contribute to what they are 'buying,'" said Donald Fishbein, a senior biotech and pharmaceutical executive. Mr. Fishbein went on to say that the type of knowledge found here enhances a business professional's ability to communicate the "why" throughout their organization. He said, "If only I had read this at the start of my career!"

Lots of people are creative, and most have the potential to think creatively (put a twist on things or see things anew) or even imaginatively—think of original ideas or things. The value of outstanding creative work produced by art directors, creative directors, copywriters, designers, and brand designers is that it is not born just out of "talent," but out of strategic creative thinking. I say "outstanding" creative work because there's a lot of average work being conceived and commercialized for a variety of reasons. This book will help you see what constitutes outstanding solutions that employ strategic creativity.

If you are sued, you are better off being represented by an attorney. I suppose there are people who represent themselves in court. Hmm. Sadly, there are loads of people who are not graphic designers who design their own websites.

This book will teach you how to get what you need from creative professionals. This is not an attempt to equate years of creative studies to a one-volume book, but it is a field guide to idea generation, creativity, copywriting, branding, graphic design, the creative side of advertising, diversity, inclusion, equity, and building a culture for results.

What Constitutes Strategic Creativity and What Doesn't

Together, you and I will explore what constitutes strategic creativity. Right off, it involves C.H.O.I.C.E. Thinking—housed within the idea, *there ought to be some emotional or functional (practical) benefit for people*, otherwise they will not pay attention or will tune out. There's too much going on 24/7 for anyone today to mind what a brand has to say if there's nothing in it for them or for someone they care about. C.H.O.I.C.E. is an acronym for Context,

Humanistic, Observational, Interesting, Craft, and Empathy. I'll explain more in Chapter 2.

Likewise, the worthwhile nature of strategic creativity falls within (or close to) **S.U.I.T.E.S. of Benefits**. The S.U.I.T.E.S. of Benefits are social good, utility, information, temptation, entertainment, and shareworthy. Of course, I will explain more about this throughout the book.

When I was a consultant to a CMO at a national beverage company, providing a second opinion on the ad campaign they were getting from their agency, I explained why the creative solutions they were getting from their agency weren't working. The CMO asked me, "Would you be willing to teach my marketing team about what constitutes getting it right?"

"I would love to," I replied. "Caveat: I'd also like to explain to them the consequences of getting it wrong."

> **It is more expensive to be safe than it is to be brave.**
> —*Jake Yrastorza, Managing Partner, Gigil*

When you don't employ strategic creativity, you run the greatest risk—a pedestrian solution that draws a big yawn from the target audience, if they notice it at all. The riskiest idea is the one people will *not* notice. If people don't notice, then there are no sales, no growth, no earned media, no buzz. Nada.

There are lots of poor options out there—poor ideas, harebrained ideas, off-brand ideas, copycat solutions, safe "we did this before, so let's do it again" ones, formulaic ideas, meh designs, dull copywriting, pedestrian art direction, uninspiring brand stories, wrong concepts for the audience, poor executions, and the biggest sin of all—damaging ideas and executions.

Employ an Effectiveness Scale

1 = Destructive or negative: The solutions hurt the company, the brand, the entity, or society
2 = Un-noticed/pedestrian: Nothing destructive, except that you've wasted money and won't get promoted
3 = Decent idea/decent execution: Doesn't build the brand; doesn't get you promoted

4   = Creative: Gets some buzz but doesn't build growth

5   = Strategically creative: Gets the brand right; gets the audience right; builds equity and growth; earns media attention; more likely to earn a promotion or a Clio.

From my years of research, teaching in higher ed, working in the creative disciplines, and working as a consultant to CMOs, brands, ad agencies, and brand studios, I'm here to offer a guided tour of strategic creativity. To get it right, come with me.

Quickstart Field Guide to Strategic Creativity

What follows are thirteen pointers so you can get started and get back to work feeling empowered. If you were hoping for a luckier number, say fourteen pointers, please feel free to add one yourself. And if you do, please let me know what you added; I'd like to make this a conversation.

1. *Strategic Creativity is* C.H.O.I.C.E. *Thinking.*

   Attention is valuable. To grab and keep people's attention, any graphic design, branding, or advertising solution must be strategically creative.

   Creative solutions are interesting. Strategically creative solutions are relevant and resonate.

   Strategic creativity relies on C.H.O.I.C.E. Thinking:

   - Context (fits into people's lives, appropriate perspective)
   - Humanistic thinking (people-centered thinking, altruistic)
   - Observation (based on an insight into people's behaviors)
   - Interesting solutions (appealing, attention-grabbing)
   - Craft (skillful execution of the idea)
   - Empathy (compassionate, identification with others)

   Strategically creative ideas and solutions move the needle from relevance to essential. Ask: Does the creative solution surprise you? Does it cut through? Is it relevant to its audience? Will it change the conversation? Call people to action?

2. *Becoming Strategically Creative.*

   Strategic creativity is the power to conceive something that solves a problem, anticipates issues, aims empathetically and appropriately at the target audience, and ultimately benefits people.

   In Chapter 3, you'll find an explanation of the S.U.I.T.E.S. of Benefits, which are **s**ocial good, **u**tility, **i**nformation, **t**emptation, **e**ntertainment, and whether a solution is **s**hareworthy.

3. *It's All About the Audience.*

   People purchase products and services to meet basic needs. Beyond that, they're purchasing fantasies. Every brand sells a fantasy—the ideal this or that, a personal or societal transformation of some kind.

   Who is the audience? Demographic? Psychographic? What are their pastimes? Which social media platforms do they use most often? Where do they shop? Where do they vacation? What do they spend their money on? What are they saying about the brand on social media? What does the data reveal?

   I asked Dr. Fred M. Feinberg, Handleman Professor and Area Chair of Marketing at Ross School of Business and Professor of Statistics in the Department of Statistics at the University of Michigan, "Why are insights into the audience important?" Dr. Feinberg replied,

   > In Marketing, we often teach that advertising can reach the wrong people with the wrong message at the wrong time: a triple mistake. But, with proper targeting and 'psychographic' insight, messages can be crafted that resonate with the specific potential customers a firm believes will find its products or services most appealing ... if they could just learn they exist and what benefits they offer. If you're selling a car to new parents, for example, almost all will find information and imagery about safety important; but, for some, money may also be tight, so reliability and fuel economy could be more powerful motivators. But that wouldn't make sense for a Mercedes-Benz® S-Class or Lamborghini®, obviously.

4. *Have a Handle on the Creative Brief and Brand Strategy.*

   The creative or design brief sets the strategy, goals, and objectives. The brief will delineate *the issue*; it's your "purpose" guide. If it seems vague, ask penetrating questions or try to rewrite it if that helps you better understand the campaign goals.

What differentiates an idea from its competition to build a relevant connection with its audience? What value does the brand offer? How can it become an absolutely can't-live-without-this brand?

Can you turn the strategy into a three-sentence story?

The consumer wants _____.

The obstacle to getting what the consumer wants is _____.

This brand can facilitate what the consumer wants because _____

_____.

5. *Worship the Insight.*

   Realize an insight into the target audience's behaviors and perceptions. The idea generation process starts with the search for an *insight*—a revelation about a way the target audience thinks or behaves in relation to the product, service, or entity. An insight ultimately changes the way we look at a behavior or situation—a human truth or finding no one has yet noticed brought to light.

   > **Find a truth about the brand. Pair it with a truth about people.**
   > **—The Community**

   To discover an insight, you can:

   Conduct social listening.
   Do small-scale field research.
   Look at it from the audience's POV.
   Build audience personas.
   Be empathetic.
   Observe people.
   Synthesize all you find.

6. *Align with Drivers of Human Behavior.*

   Human behavior is first and foremost a kind of "investment." Individuals do what they do because of either implicit or explicit benefits directed at desired outcomes. Ask: How does your ad idea serve the audience's self-interest?

In Chapter 6, you'll read about some of the major drivers of human behavior, which are survival, pleasure, safety, belonging, love, sex, acquisition, status, rivalry, power, safety, convenience, enrichment, and thrills.

7. *Go with Strategically Creative Ideas. Kill the Pedestrian Ones.*

An idea can change the way people think about a brand, entity, cause, issue, or individual. It can offer proof, create desire, or stir an emotion that imprints the message. An idea can reframe a conversation, do some social good, taunt a competitor, empower, motivate, endear the audience, or simply entertain.

A strategically creative idea must A.L.T.E.R. people's thinking:

Attract: People must notice it and find it appealing enough to talk about it or share it.
Lodestar: It must have a "lodestar" idea—the central premise, mission, and guiding light—that makes each execution conceptually sound.
Timely: Ideas should be opportune, well timed, appropriate, and judicious.
Engage: It should be involving, interesting, or stimulating, or it should prompt or move people to do something. Tell a story. *Provide a hero's journey.*
Resonate: People should find it remarkable, relatable, and relevant to their aspirations and desires. Ideally, it should respond to their hopes or needs to resonate.

Ask: Would your idea make people think or feel something? Change their point of view? Always remember to ask: *What's the overarching Lodestar idea?*

8. *Think Like a Copywriter.*

To think like a copywriter, keep these three objectives in mind: 1) How fresh phrases or sentences can grab someone's attention, 2) Communicating a clear takeaway message to the right people, and 3) Gauging whatever you're saying/writing from the audience's perspective. The reader should think: "Oh yeah, that's so true!" or "You know me."

9. *Think Like a Designer.*

To think like a designer, keep these three objectives in mind: 1) How the design elements and principles work to communicate, 2) Attracting the people you're aiming at and keeping their visual interest, and

3) Differentiating the brand or entity through individual design solutions and across the program or campaign.

Check for balance, a visual hierarchy (arrangement of graphic elements according to importance), unity, rhythm, interesting shape relationships and a compelling graphic space, and an appropriate voice expressed through typeface selection and treatment.

Design makes the solution cohesive, flow, and accessible. Are the design principles acting to visually communicate?

10. *Think Like a Brand Storyteller.*

To think like a brand storyteller, consider two main aspects of crafting the underlying concept for a brand story that will resonate. First, the brand narrative must align with the brand's values and actions. Sounds like a no-brainer; however, many companies think they can say something but not back it up with actions. Second, the brand narrative and each story told must align with a driver of human behavior.

11. *Art Direction Creates an Indelible Point of View.*

To think like an art director, consider how to best communicate the ad idea to the right audience through the cooperative relationship of copy and image; the style of visualization; the emphasis of the headline or the image; the brand voice as expressed through the imagery, style, and typography; and how to organize all of it to capture people's attention.

How do the color palette, imagery, typeface, layout, and style all convey the idea and message and appropriate tone? Is the idea visualized in a unique way that enhances the brand voice?

Each execution in a campaign should ladder up to the Lodestar idea for the campaign.

12. *Respect: Diversity, Equity, and Inclusion.*

Professionals who create and distribute pop culture artifacts have a responsibility to be a force for good and to build trust. Commit yourself to uplifting all members of society, including those of different races, ethnicities, genders, sexualities, religions, beliefs, ages, and abilities.

Have you interrogated the idea, images, and copy for meaning?

Who holds the power in the portrayal?

Is another's narrative or culture being employed? Is it yours to appropriate?

Nothing in pop culture happens in a vacuum. Do No Harm.

13. *Building a Culture for Results.*

For creative collaboration to happen, people must trust and respect each other. Trust is earned through respect, transparency, and diplomacy.

To build strategic creative communication, the team generates ideas through civil discourse and exchange.

Use the improv method of "Yes, and ..." to allow one team member to build on another's thoughts. Work towards shared goals and trust each participant's expertise.

It's best to persistently build a workplace culture for strategically creative results.

Interview with REI INAMOTO, Founding Partner of I&CO

Figure 1.1 Rei Inamoto
Photographer: Jeong Park

Named in *Creativity* magazine's annual "Creativity 50" as well as one of the "Top 25 Most Creative People in Advertising" in *Forbes* magazine, Rei Inamoto is one of the most influential individuals in the marketing and creative industry today.

Until the fall of 2015, Rei served as Chief Creative Officer of AKQA, responsible for delivering creative solutions for the agency's worldwide clients, such as Audi®, Google®, Nike®, Xbox®, and many others. During his tenure, AKQA grew tenfold, expanding to a network of 14 offices across the world. It also became the first agency in history to receive five Agency of the Year accolades from industry publications .

In early 2016, Rei—along with Rem Reynolds—founded I&CO, a business invention firm that identifies new opportunities and creates best-in-class customer experiences by focusing on strategy, design, and incubation. The *Fast Company* annual named I&CO one of the Most Innovative Companies in the World. In July of 2019, I&CO opened its first international office in Tokyo.

Rei is a frequent speaker at numerous conferences as well as a contributor to publications, making him a thought leader and a prominent voice in the industry.

Originally from Tokyo, Rei spent his childhood and teenage years in Japan and Europe. He then moved to the US to complete his university studies with degrees in fine arts and computer science.

He currently resides in Brooklyn, New York.

You've written four laws of brand-building in the digital age. What should clients and other business experts understand about your thinking?

The main thing is to let go of your past thinking and be willing to pivot the way you approach brand-building. The following are recent shifts I have noticed:

1. From Organizational Scale to Functional Speed

    Your team does not need to be small to be fast. "Functional speed" is the ability to accelerate or decelerate when it matters the most. Take what happened in the video conferencing space in 2020— Zoom® became a household name, but shortly after Google turned on its functional speed to challenge Zoom. Google, by acknowledging the users' needs and updating its product immediately, exercised their functional speed.

2. From Original Selling (USP) to Point of View (POV)

    USP has been, for a long time, the golden rule of marketing and branding. In the twenty-first century, the importance of POV has risen significantly. USP might give you an edge for a little while, but it's only a matter of time before your USP is copied by someone else. A strong POV will remind you why you started in the first place.

3. From Case Study to Business Case

    The role of a case study is to show off an outcome in the best possible way—for example, when entering work for award shows.

A business case is created to define the value a project will deliver. To make the best case, consider looking past the aesthetics of a case study and into the truths of a strong business case.

4. From Ideal Futures to Practical Futures

We help clients answer the question, "How should I be thinking about the future of my business?" When planning for the future, the further away the time horizon is, the more speculative your plan becomes. It might sound good on paper and in meetings but not be realistic in practice. On the other hand, creating an immediate, probable future won't make your business competitive enough. What we call a "practical future" is a time span close enough to the present to be achievable but far enough away to allow for ambition to thrive. The goal is always to deliver a lasting and meaningful impact.

What's the best route for clients to get meaningful solutions and what you term "practical futures" from their agencies?

Be ambitious and be practical at the same time.

What should everyone in the advertising and brand-building business understand about establishing a distinguishable and strong point of view?

There are two questions you should always be thinking about:

1. What differentiates you from others?
2. Why do you do what you do as a company/brand?

Have you found a way to foster an appreciation for great art direction and copy in clients or in other business people involved with making decisions about creative solutions?

The person at the top needs to have an appreciation for aesthetics and craft. Otherwise, it'll be an uphill battle.

Often account or marketing folks might appreciate what you did for one brand and ask you to create something similar for their brand. Can you provide an argument against this ask?

The purpose of marketing is to highlight how you are different from others. So doing something similar unfortunately isn't going to help you.

Individuals don't always recognize how their taste is affecting their judgement about an agency's creative solution. What's a workable way for clients and business people to approach and analyze a creative advertising or brand solution presented to them?

It's important to have someone on your team who's experienced in providing feedback with creative solutions and learning from them.

Why is it important for everyone in advertising to aim for diversity, equity, and inclusion?

Externally, these considerations should be built into the work because we produce work that has the power to influence culture. Internally, these conversations need to happen to build a better workplace.

What should everyone in the advertising and brand-building business understand about cultural appropriation?

Appropriation is rooted in power and privilege:

- Be aware of generalizations/stereotyping by frequently checking your biases.
- You can't ignore cultural significance, so you must do your research and credit your sources.
- Ultimately, execution must match intent.

How can clients and business experts productively and diplomatically discuss creative solutions with the creative team, agency CCO, or agency founder (such as yourself)?

1. Be open.
2. Be a team.
3. Care.

You told Amanda Smiley of The Drum that to be a great creative professional, you follow three key mantras: "There's a way, always"; "Quality is a habit"; and "When in doubt, subtract." What would your suggested three key mantras be for clients, CEOs, COOs, and marketing professionals?

I would say the same three mantras to clients, CEOs, COOs, and marketing professionals. There is always a need to think with a creative mindset because creativity is not limited to those with creative titles.

When a client doesn't know exactly what they want, what's the best way for them to discuss their objectives with you or your creative teams?

It's okay not to know what you want—just be open about it.

Why should clients and other participating business people support a creative team's solution that might be something atypical, daring, or new?

One of the guiding maxims at I&CO is "Risk nothing, change nothing." Taking a risk often makes us uncomfortable. It's natural to go the other way. But comfort leads to complacency. Complacency leads to stagnation, which is the exact opposite of change.

The only other option to taking a risk is not taking any. And without taking one at all, there is no progress. That is precisely the biggest risk of all.

What are five aspects of the creative side of advertising and brand-building you wish business professionals (business owners, CEOs, clients, marketing teams) understood? Please explain.

1. Creativity should belong to everyone.

    One of the most pivotal organizational inventions of this industry was the art director/copywriter team pairing conceived by Bill Bernbach back in the 1960s. This was quite effective for a long time. It also had a detrimental effect in that it created an elitist atmosphere among so-called creatives and an unintended submissive position for the rest. It's now time to debunk this stance: demand creativity from everyone in your company and dethrone creative elitism. Creativity no longer belongs to only creatives.

2. Quality is a habit.

    "Beware the lollipop of mediocrity; lick it once and you'll suck forever," said Brian Wilson of the Beach Boys. Apparently, it only takes 21 days for something to become a habit. Put another way, it only takes 21 days for compromise to become a habit. You don't want to get used to sacrificing quality. It's a slippery slope.

3. When in doubt, subtract.

    "Make it simple" is easy to say but hard to do. So how do we make things simple? The temptation to add more creeps up when we aren't sure. Adding more will lead to more complexity. Resist that temptation. Simplicity always trumps complexity.

4. Communication or advertising no longer builds a brand as effectively as it once did.

   The algorithm of advertising—come up with the so-called Big Idea, sell a product based on it, and hope it'll build a brand—has now become a thing of the past. Think of other ways to build a brand.

Note

1 "McCann Romania Puts 'Dr. Internet' to the Test to Tackle Self Diagnosis," *Little Black Book*. June 5, 2019. https://www.lbbonline.com/news/mccann-romania-puts-dr-internet-to-the-test-to-tackle-self-diagnosis.

Advertising is more than just being able to reference other ads. The best ideas are born from curiosity—being interested in many different things like art, history, nature, people, culture. It's coming to the table with those different perspectives, life experiences, and interests that help us get inspired. And the most exciting part about inspiration is that you never know where it'll come from next.

—*Christine Gratton, Creative Director*

Chapter

Thinking Creatively

The Power of Strategic Creativity

I felt a tug on my nightshirt.

"Mom, I had a bad dream," my daughter Hayley said.

"My poor baby," I replied and carried Hayley back to her bed. "Let's see if I can help you get back to sleep and have pleasant dreams."

According to the Cleveland Clinic, an estimated 10% to 50% of children aged three to six years old have nightmares that can seem "terrifyingly real."[1] The exact cause of nightmares is not known, according to the Mayo Clinic and the Cleveland Clinic. However, there are ways to help a child cope and reduce the risk of having bad dreams.

After two nights of bad dreams resulting in significant sleep disturbance and distress for my daughter, my husband, and myself, I conducted casual research and generated a potential solution.

"This is a dream box," I said to Hayley and opened a box, which was a tea box that I had covered with wrapping paper. "Tell your nightmare to the dream box. Then, close the lid and I'll put the dream box away. You won't have any more bad dreams," I said to my daughter.

Hayley did as I asked. She then said, "How does it work?"

"It's magic. It just does."

At Hayley's age of three years old, magical thinking still worked. Kids at that age believe in magical notions, such as the tooth fairy. The dream box idea worked for Hayley, so I turned it into a children's book to help other families as well. Disguised as a picture book, *The Dream Box* helps solve a real-life, common dilemma—what to do when a child has a bad dream.

I employed strategic creativity to solve my family's problem.

C.H.O.I.C.E. Thinking

Strategic creativity is the power to create something that solves a problem, aims empathetically and appropriately at the target audience, and ultimately benefits people. Let's look through that lens.

DOI: 10.4324/9781003230786-2

Using strategic creativity to address the issue of nightmares, I considered that the solution should be *contextual* (the day-to-day role in someone's life, someone's routine); *humanistic* (decent, ethical, principled, believing you can make a change, activist, advocate, or supporting of reform); *observational* (everything is content and content is everything); *interesting* (you have to capture people's attention and keep it to communicate with them); *crafted well* (well thought out; an execution good enough to engage people); and, *empathetic* (responsive, compassionate).

> **Creativity is not a talent. It is a way of operating.**
> **—John Cleese**

Cleese is correct. What follows is C.H.O.I.C.E. Thinking plus a series of prompts intended to enhance creativity.

C.H.O.I.C.E. Thinking plus Creative Prompts

Context / Humanistic / Observational / Interesting / Craft / Empathy

C for Context

How does your solution fit into people's daily lives, their routines? How does it inspire people to meet their goals or live their best lives? When people feel a solution is doing more than what is necessary to get by, they react more positively and become more frequent users, increasing loyalty and sales.

Prompts

Re-routing

What would encourage people to take a different route to work—a more scenic or interesting route? What would encourage them to walk or bike part of the way, if possible? Or how could you encourage people to change their morning or evening routines?

Brush, Brush, Brush

What exercise movements could people do while brushing their teeth?

H for Humanistic

This one is straightforward—is the solution compassionate? Benevolent? Does the solution add to positive things in the world, or does it do harm? When it comes to a brand, entity, or individual, how conscientious, ethical, or humanistic should it be in action and communication?

Prompts

Take a Walk In Someone Else's ...

Shoes. Reconceive an ending to a classic folklore story, fairy tale, or classic film from a supporting or minor character's point of view.

Authentic Kindness

What's one thing a brand or company could do to be kinder? How does it fit into the brand or entity's mission, values, and beliefs?

If Only:

If only this brand_____ would_____.

I wish this organization would or did_____.

O for Observation

Everything is content.

Pay close attention to things—your environment, conversations, behaviors, motifs—everything that surrounds you. Whether you're an observational comedian, such as Michelle Buteau, a physicist, such as Richard Feynman, or a marketing executive, employ the power of observation. One day, while in the cafeteria, "Some guy, fooling around, throws a plate in the air,"[2] writes Richard Feynman in his book, *Surely You're Joking, Mr. Feynman!* By observing how the plate spun—noting the difference between the plate's angular velocity and its wobble motion—Feynman realized something: "The diagrams and the whole business that I got the Nobel Prize for came from that piddling around with the wobbling plate."

Interesting

One more time: Everything is content.

Having your finger on the pulse of pop culture is critical to staying sharp. Paying attention to pop culture, cultural events, trends, and the news feeds creative thinking. Figuring out how it applies to what your audience is interested in and how they can participate with your brand or entity is what makes it strategic creative thinking.

Appealing to more than one sense offers a better chance of imprinting on someone, of moving someone. Ask, does an advertising, branding, or a design solution excite or engage people's senses? If you consider the success of a song or the dance challenges that use music, lyrics, and dance on TikTok®—a platform rooted in music and dance—to stir people to participate, you can see the appeal of a multisensory approach. With the #eyeslipsface TikTok challenge, agency Movers+Shakers helped beauty brand e.l.f.® jump from No. 8 to the No. 2 favorite beauty brand among Gen Z, and the brand experienced eight consecutive quarters of sales growth.[3]

> **Successful advertising makes use of research, data, institutional knowledge, and strategic insight. But none of those essential elements matter until creativity comes along to bind them into something consumers can laugh with, love with, or want to live their lives with.**
> **—Greg Braun, retired Dep.,**
> **Global Chief Creative Officer of**
> **Commonwealth/McCann**

Prompts

Ambient Thinking

Turn an environment or an object found in a built environment into something else, for instance, a tree stump into a pop-up book or a baggage claim carousel into a roulette wheel.

Sound and Lights

What could you create for TikTok (or another platform that offers sound) or an event that could offer other sense experiences, such as taste, that you can't do in a static digital or print ad or design?

C is for Craft

When I took an advertising course with ad agency principal Sal DeVito, he employed categories to critique our work. Three of the telling categories were: "Good Idea/Poor Execution," "Poor Idea/Good Execution," and "Great Idea/Great Execution."

Let's always aim for the third: "Great Idea/Great Execution."

Prompts

That's a Thing

Think of something "That's a Thing"—a trend, an object, or something people are doing that's a recent phenomenon. For example: Pizza vending machines. Vegan condoms. No periods after text messages. Extreme squirreling. Doom scrolling.

Hack Pop Culture

Identify something in pop culture that you could hack for a brand or entity. For instance: A meme. Something that happened at the Grammy Awards. The latest action film or the latest film flop. Celebrity relationships. Mock or embrace the musical theater genre.

E for Empathetic

Lead with empathy.

Design thinking—a human-centered approach to thinking about and designing solutions to problems—relies a great deal upon empathy.

I invoke Design Thinking here because it's human-centered, starting with a deep empathy of people and an understanding of their motivations, desires, and needs. It is also reflective, intentional, and iterative.

Prompts

Anti-Valentine's Day

In the US, there are a lot of single people who feel left out or lonely on Valentine's Day, a day that celebrates couples. To address that, think of an experiential marketing event for singles that would offer a fun thing to do on Valentine's Day. Tie it to an appropriate brand, if possible.

> **Design thinking is a method of problem-solving that relies on a complex set of skills, processes, and mindsets that help people generate novel solutions to problems. Design thinking can result in new objects, ideas, narratives, or systems. The excitement over design thinking lies in the proposition that anyone can learn to do it. The democratic promise of design thinking is that once design thinking has been mastered anyone can go about redesigning the systems, infrastructures, and organizations that shape our lives.**
> *—Shelley Goldman, Stanford School of Education, and Zaza Kabayadondo, Design Thinking Initiative at Smith College*

Aspiration List

Make a list of ten things you aspire to and ten things you believe your best mate aspires to as well. See if there's any crossover. Do you think most people aspire to some of the same things, for instance, achieving a personal best?

Hack: Ask, "What Else Can I Do with This?"

To combat a pattern or an assumed tendency, ask yourself, "What else can I do with this?" It might lead to discoveries.

- What else can you do with a paper plate besides eat on it?
- What else (thing or notion) is as layered as an onion?

- A courtroom: Change the frame.
- Think of a convention and turn it on its head.
- Observe: Watch different people eat a sandwich.
- What would a slacker do? What would a type-A do?
- Could a leaf sub as a paintbrush?
- Tell a story backward (think Harold Pinter's play *Betrayal*).

Courage

Some people default to pedestrian solutions because they find them safe, or they fear failure, or they fear appearing foolish for saying or suggesting something divergent. My advice: Carry a pineapple. Everywhere you go. People might stare at you, but you'll get over the fear of appearing foolish.

> **The opposite of courage is not cowardice. The opposite of courage is conformity.**
> —*Brian Collins, chief creative officer, COLLINS*

Creative is as creative does. When I asked Mike Felix, Creative Director at DDB New Zealand, to advise about creative thinking, he said, "You can't write a quote arguing for creativity. If you were really being creative, you'd find a more effective way to get your point across."

The Strategic Creativity Effectiveness Scale

A couple of prominent ad agencies, such as Leo Burnett and FCB, use effectiveness scales or ladders to judge creative solutions. Here's one you can employ.

1. Negative: This does harm; the solution impacts negatively on people, society, culture, the brand, or entity. For more information, please read Chapter 7. Harming the brand or entity can happen in a variety of ways as well.
2. Undistinguishable: No one is going to notice it because it is not differentiated, it is a pedestrian idea, or it is a retread.
3. Not on brand: Misses the brand's mission or purpose or voice.
4. Not a strategically creative idea: This idea (or lack of) will not build the brand.
5. On brand and purpose but not attention-getting.

6. Attention-getting in the short term.

7. Strategic creativity: Builds the brand or entity in the long term. Calls people to action. Changes people's behavior or thinking.

Interview with RICK COSGROVE, President of Agency EA

Figure 2.1 Rick Cosgrove
Photographer: Jon Shaft

As President of Agency EA, Rick Cosgrove leads the overall management and growth of the business through strategy and direction across the client services, production, and creative departments. Rick began his tenure at EA in 2010, evolving from the agency's first in-house designer to incepting the Creative Department in 2014 and building it to a team of 45 spanning across strategy, graphic and spatial design, copywriting, and digital. With a background in architecture and an MBA from Northwestern's Kellogg School of Management, Rick brings a balanced approach to creating exceptional experiences and managing the teams that bring them to life. If you hear "ticking" coming from his office, don't worry—it's just his collection of clocks.

What are five points you wish business professionals (business owners, CEOs, clients, marketing teams) understood about the creative side of advertising, experiential marketing, branding, and design? Please explain.

When creatives begin work on a program, they're trying to simultaneously: represent existing brand language and identity, bring a fresh approach based on the brief, and take feedback that may be convolutive or contradictive, all while trying to remain within budgeted hours to execute the work. It is an incredibly difficult job. Here are a few considerations that will build a strong relationship across any group of creatives:

1. Remember that most creatives do care far more about the brand's success than industry awards.
2. Build a brief worth framing with impeccable insights, a clear target and objective, and honest criteria for execution and evaluation expectations.
3. Try to critique creative concepts through the lens of the end audience; don't let personal subjective tastes drive direction.
4. Ensure clarity on which individual within the brand team will make final decisions and meet feedback deadlines.
5. They're an extension of your brand, so make them feel like a teammate, not a vendor.

What should business professionals, business owners, and clients understand about the creative conception and execution of in-person promotional experiences, such as events, product showcases, branded conferences, and pop-up activations?

Building a live/virtual experience takes a massive amount of effort from multiple experts: strategists, designers, technology experts, content builders, copywriters, budget managers, show callers, fabricators, etc., etc. The list goes on as the complexities build.

There will always be hiccups and on-site challenges that need fast resolutions. The best agencies will let you know how they resolved an issue before you knew there was one. The worst ones will tell you there isn't time to fix it.

What should B2B companies consider when hiring an experiential agency and evaluating creative solutions?

All agencies are structured differently, and it's worth understanding how work will flow through your future project team when you're looking for an experiential partner. For example, who works on the RFPs [Requests for Proposals] and who will be on the live project phase? How is the creative team structured and what members are in-house vs. contracted? Are they hiring any additional agencies to work on the project under their management? The list goes on because live experiential work has many layers and vendor partnerships to bring a show to life.

Don't start at the bottom line of the budget. Read the response in full and figure out which agency really understands what is needed for a flawless execution of whatever concept is ultimately agreed upon. I remember once we lost a bid for a massive product launch because we came in $800K higher than our competitor. We clearly explained that whatever they proposed to build, this massive LED structure was not accurate as it would require a superstructure to properly hold it in place. Sure enough, after the event finished and we reconnected with the client, we heard they went over budget by $1.2M.

Look beyond the concepts themselves and see if the agency has given you a "why." Without this, they may only be cool ideas that lack a purposeful strategy for the brand.

If you were to give a speed workshop in experiential design and marketing, what three tenets would you emphasize?

1. Start in the clouds for the big idea and quickly come down to the ground. Live experiences and events require serious coordination between creative, budget management, and production execution.
2. Engagement requires active participation. If you want authentic connections between people and brands, you must create an environment that initiates and facilitates participation. Passive viewing limits both attention span and emotional connections.
3. Cohesion is key—from the first marketing touchpoints to the registration page, pre-event comms, the on-site experience, the general session content, the evening events, networking sessions, and post-event surveys and comms. Consistency means a clear event brand guideline and a team with attention to detail.

Is there a benefit to hybrid events? What should business executives and clients consider when deciding on an in-person, hybrid, or fully remote promotional experience?

One thing is certain: people are now far more comfortable with a virtual session or broadcast than they were before 2020. Knowing this, a calendar of events can include both in-person and virtual events. The most successful brands will be taking their goals and questioning: "What must be done physically, what can be done virtually, and what requires a fully inclusive hybrid model to maximize the total audience?" There is no doubt that most brands will end up with a balance of in-person, hybrid, and fully remote experiences within a given year.

1. Start with the full list of essential brand experiences for the year.
2. Cross reference the audience-reach goals and necessary messaging.
3. From there, assess the format (physical, virtual, or hybrid) to maximize the specific metrics for success on that program.

So much of what you decide regarding format is dependent on your core audience profile. Who are you trying to reach? What's the total quantity of that audience? Where is the majority of that audience located? Is it easy for that audience to take time off work and travel to the event location for a few days? Is it possible for the show/experience itself to travel to different cities? Are the concepts you want to showcase easily transferable to the virtual space? The list of assessment questions goes on, but ultimately the budgetary and event goals will allow you to weigh the ideal audience outcomes appropriately against the format options.

Any best practices for business people on working with creative teams and agencies?

Be specific and give tight parameters. Most people assume creatives enjoy unfettered freedom when designing. The real challenge is taking specific parameters and concepting within those boundaries, so the result successfully hits the objectives.

Don't feel the need to filter everything through the client service team. Feedback should elicit a discussion, and if you're only sharing it with your account lead, you'll miss out on possibly sparking the best ideas in a collaborative way.

Scope creep: acknowledge it before the agency mentions it first. It's never comfortable for an agency that's trying to build a relationship to address when the ask is outside the originally agreed deliverable.

It's a partnership. The agency is doing everything it can to provide the brand with an incredible product. Brand leads should do everything they can to support the agency back. Be on time with feedback, make decisions in a timely manner, recognize when budgets need to increase, and ultimately, be kind. Agencies know who's paying the bill—don't wield that power in a negative way.

Agency EA is a full-service brand experience agency. What's your philosophy about connecting brands with their target audiences?

Most of Agency EA's work lies in B2B experiences, so our goals are rooted in the three-pronged value creation between customers, collaborators, and the company (brand) that's hosting the experience. The key in the B2B experiential space is to create an environment where maximum value is created for all three.

1. Customers (the main audience) gain value from exposure to the company's thought leadership, opportunities to network with other customers, and access to collaborator offerings.
2. Collaborators (other brands) should gain value from the host brand's partnership and the exposure to the customers they otherwise may not have reached.
3. The company gains value by expanding its brand presence, growing authentic ties to its core audience, strengthening its partnerships with collaborators, and, ideally, building brand community after the event ends.

How does experiential branding align with a brand's overall architecture and contribute to the overall brand narrative?

Upon kicking off any new program in the experiential space, designers ideally want to gauge where the program's identity, tone, and voice falls across an imaginary sliding scale between the strict corporate brand ID and an essentially blank slate. There is typically a distinct correlation between the desired audience (customers, partner brands, internal employees, investors, etc.) to determine where the "dot" lands across that scale. Is this experience a one-off or will it repeat year after year? Ultimately, what needs to be decided is if the goal is to build a sub-brand that has its own unique identity that ladders to the master brand (think Google vs. I/O®), a literal extension of the existing identity, or something wholly separate and unique from the parent brand.

Any advice for business people on how not to kill a creative idea and proposal?

Creative results that resonate well with clients typically started with an equally strong creative brief. If you find the results of an agency's creative proposal are missing the mark, go back to your original directive. Were you clear on your target and the purpose of the experience? Was there clarity on how closely the creative should reflect or deviate from the brand's current positioning? What criteria/weight is being used to evaluate the work? By spending time building the strongest brief possible prior to enlisting an agency to work on behalf of a brand, there is a greater likelihood that the creative ideas presented will have resonance.

How can people who are not trained in the visual arts best understand what makes for an effective design, branding, or ad solution? How can you foster an appreciation of art direction in someone who is not a visual artist?

Start with intent.

If a person with no appreciation for art goes to a museum, they will still, if asked, share their opinions on what they liked based on their own subjective aesthetic preferences.

Now imagine if, prior to entering the museum, that same individual was given context to each artist's intention and a list of objective questions to ponder on while viewing the work. Likely the assessment would be much different.

Get into a habit of asking contextual questions prior to casting judgement on design work—understand the "what" and "why" behind the design decisions that were made. From there it is much easier to give objective feedback that may lead to stronger iterations. Ultimately, everyone has opinions on what they like, dislike, and are indifferent on, but the more we strive to understand context and intent, the easier it is for a non-visual person to give meaningful feedback.

Here's a fun tactic to help build confidence in a non-visual person's ability to assess work. Share two different restaurant menus: one that is poorly designed and copywritten and one that was purposefully designed. Ask the person which one they'd rather eat at. After they choose the well-designed menu (hopefully they do), get their rationale on what drove their decision and share explanations on what tactics were behind the design decisions made on the better menu.

Notes

1   "Nightmares in Children," *Cleveland Clinic*. September 9, 2020. https://my.clevelandclinic.org/health/articles/14297-nightmares-in-children.
2   Richard Feynman, *Surely You're Joking, Mr. Feynman!: Adventures of a Curious Character*. London: Vintage Books. 1992.
3   "From the 13th Annual Shorty Awards: e.l.f. Cosmetics' Innovation on TikTok," *Shorty Awards*. 2020. https://shortyawards.com/13th/elf-cosmetics-innovation-on-tiktok.

Creative insights don't happen on demand.
They come on their own schedule after much
incubation of related ideas. So don't expect
creative folks to be able to tell you what they will
come up with and when. They dance to a different
beat and a different drummer. But give them lots of
relevant information, and deadlines with a fair amount
of lead time.

—Ajay K. Kohli, Gary T. and Elizabeth R. Jones
Chair in Management, Regents Professor, Georgia Tech

Chapter

3

Strategically Creative Ideas

What's In It For Me?

In one of Bill Watterson's *Calvin and Hobbes* cartoon strips, Calvin, the little boy, answers the phone. The caller asks to speak to Calvin's father. When Calvin responds that his father is not home, the caller then asks if Calvin would please take a message. Calvin replies, "What's in it for me?"

Strategically creative ideas do more than sell a product or service once. They offer a **benefit**; align with people's **aspirations**, desires, or needs as well as with the brand or entity's core **narrative construct**; are **ownable** within the construct; and are **fresh**. A strategic creative idea might even **change the way someone thinks, feels, or acts**, allowing them to see a different viewpoint, scenario, or outcome. Let's aim for strategic creativity and kill the pedestrian ideas.

S.U.I.T.E.S. of Benefits

"What's in it for me?"

Housed within the idea, *there ought to be some emotional or functional (practical) benefit for people*, otherwise they will not pay attention or will tune out. There's too much going on 24/7 today for anyone to mind what a brand has to say if there's nothing in it for them or for someone they care about. Likely, the worth falls within (or close to) the S.U.I.T.E.S. of Benefits, which you will recall from the Quickstart Field Guide in Chapter 1.

The S.U.I.T.E.S. of Benefits are:

- *Social good*: Something that aids a great number of people in the realm of safety, health, community, education, the environment, and so on.
- *Utility*: Something useful—an app, a calculator, a guide, and so on—digital or physical.
- *Information*: Some knowledge or content that reports, enlightens, advises, or educates.
- *Temptation*: An appeal, inducement, or enticement, perhaps the lure of excitement.

DOI: 10.4324/9781003230786-3

- *Entertainment*: Content that provides enjoyment, diversion, thrills, or amusement.
- *Shareworthy*: Relatable content, which will add to their coolness; first-to-know status; or whether people will find it original, surprising, heretical, irresistible, or just plain likeable. *Sharing is how an idea becomes a contagion.*
- All or some combo of the above.

The Promise of Fulfillment

"I Was Once A 97-Pound Weakling," read one of the headlines written by Charles Roman for Charles Atlas's company in 1928. Atlas was the original 97-pound weakling who transformed himself and brought physical fitness to America. Atlas's promise was: You, too, can transform yourself into a muscle man. That is, if you subscribe to his mail-order exercise regimen.

Does an idea promise transformation? Wish fulfillment, or satisfy a desire head-on? Does it promise to answer a need, want, aspiration, yearning for change, experimentation, or something else that is about hope or unmet desires?

Brand Narrative Construct Alignment

A clever idea might work well to sell or promote a product or service in the short term. If the creative idea isn't strategically aligned with the overall brand narrative construct, then it will not be helpful to build the brand in the long term, enhance the brand's position in the marketplace, (further) imprint the brand in the mind of the appropriate people, or keep the narrative alive and fresh.

Take purpose, proposition, and positioning into account. Understanding the purpose—why the brand, company, or organization exists—will aid differentiation. Stephen Boidock, Director of Marketing at McGarrah Jessee, advises,

> Perhaps the most important thing for a brand is to have a strong positioning. If it's good, it aligns to what the brand believes in and how it wants to exist in culture. If it's great, it helps it differentiate from others wanting to do something similar. Once the positioning is established, it should become the North Star for everything the brand does, even beyond marketing. The reality is, every touchpoint, large and small, is part of a brand experience, so making

sure your entire organization is aligned and working to bring the positioning to life is critical.

Brand Ownability

A brand construct should be "ownable," that is a position or attribute *uniquely* claimed for the brand or entity, even if others possess the same functional benefit or offer the same emotional benefit. Often, a brand or entity preempts the competition from owning a construct claim, which *grows in people's minds over time through building the brand narrative.* For example, Volvo® "owns" safety; BMW® "owns" German engineering; Jeep® "owns" adventure, although all these brands share fairly similar basic functional benefits—they get you from here to there. (Though if you're a brand loyalist, you might think there's no competitor.)

Fresh

No one notices commonplace graphic design, branding, or advertising. If it is unremarkable, no one will make remarks about it. Or share it.

Running with fresh on-brand ideas that offer a benefit and are aligned with the brand construct narrative is strategic. And smart business. No one will bother engaging with stale ideas.

Kill the pedestrian ideas and run with what people might find novel or appealing.

Behavioral Change

If an idea calls people to action or to change their behaviors, attitudes, or beliefs, or it exposes people to a new or different point of view, or if at minimum it offers the potential for a change, that exhibits strategic creative thinking. Not every strategically creative idea is a game changer; however, a strategically creative one can make people rethink things or their actions.

Strategic creative ideas create spaces for people to participate (see the interview with Rick Cosgrove in Chapter 2). They allow people to imagine how they want to be or live.

Creative campaigns perform better. This is according to the research by Les Binet and Peter Field, who have been researching marketing effectiveness for over a decade.[1] Of course, those creative campaigns are based on strategically creative ideas.

Take the Moldy WHOPPER® video, where we see Burger King®'s signature sandwich, the WHOPPER, rotting in time-lapse footage to the sound of Dinah Washington singing "What a Difference a Day Makes."

On YouTube, a viewer commented, "Someone's either about to be fired or about to be promoted."

Why show your signature product rotting? Burger King reports, "The beauty of real food is that it gets ugly. That's why we are rolling out a WHOPPER that is free from artificial preservatives. Isn't it beautiful? #NoArtificialPreservatives" (Agencies: NGO/Stockholm; DAVID/Miami; Publicis/Bucharest; Mayflower/New York).

About the Moldy WHOPPER, Fernando Machado, the former CMO of Burger King, told *Muse by Clio,*

> We understand that the biggest risk is to do something people are not going to notice or care about. We took a leap of faith and pushed the boundaries further than we normally do for BK—but for a good cause. We've been working on removing preservatives from artificial sources from our products for many years now, and we've started to reach some of the key milestones where we're comfortable talking about the changes publicly. So, we needed something special. When we saw "Moldy WHOPPER," it was love at first sight.[2]

Machado's concern—doing something people aren't going to notice—is well founded. In their research on boredom in interpersonal encounters, social psychologist Mark Leary and his three colleagues found that people can bore others either by *what* they have to say or *how* they say it: Both content and style matter.[3]

If we extend that belief to advertising, branding, and graphic design, then we must avoid pedestrian ideas. Instead, offer fresh takes and content so that people will take notice. If people are seriously shopping for big-ticket items, such as a new car or lawnmower, they are more likely to notice and read advertisements for those goods; however, it's a matter of getting them to notice the advertisement first. Conversely, getting someone who is not in the market for a car in the moment, is a much more challenging problem.

Again, the risk is in distributing boring solutions, not in strategic creative ones.

Strategic Creativity

If you have doubts about how and why creative thinking is critical, let's look at another solution for Burger King (BK)—"WHOPPER Detour."

Burger King's goal was to make ordering as convenient as possible, reboot its mobile presence, and keep up with mobile ordering. Using geofencing technology, agency FCB New York and Burger King unveiled the WHOPPER Detour, which worked when people came within 600 feet of a McDonald's® restaurant. Once people downloaded the BK app, if they drove to a McDonald's location (14,000 were geofenced across the US), they automatically received a coupon for a one-cent WHOPPER. According to Burger King, the WHOPPER Detour resulted in 1.5 million app downloads and mobile sales tripled during the promotion. After the promotion ended, Burger King continued to sell twice the amount through its app.[4]

The WHOPPER Detour campaign won tons of industry awards. Burger King fans, who were accustomed to Burger King trolling their competitor, bought in to the ultimate troll.

Become a Strategically Creative Idea Generator

Everyone can learn to generate a creative yet viable idea.

Be a True Detective. Read the Brief. Analyze the Brief. Re-read the brief and pull out the key phrases that will allow you to understand the goals and your charge. Here lies crucial audience and strategy information and perhaps an insight into the audience, brand, or competitors. If a brief is written poorly, then you need to ask questions or decipher it.

Based on the brief, it's helpful to write a one-sentence directive to guide you.

To best grasp the charge, employ the usual detective's or journalist's questions: Who? What? Why?

Answer these questions:

Who are we talking to?
What do we need to make happen?
Why are we doing this? And *why* should the target audience heed our call to action?
What is the brand's "why"—its essential lifeblood?

Renato Fernandez, CCO of TBWA\Chiat\Day Los Angeles, advises,

> Ask all the questions, even the most stupid ones. Many times, they unlock a creative truth, and that's what you should be looking for. The creative truth— that is the canvas for the creative idea. Without it, your ideas will be shallow or similar to many others out there.

Social Listening

The brief may not contain enough research or resources may be scarce. In this case, you will need to conduct your own research. If you don't have resources, the easiest route is social listening. Monitor social media platforms for mentions of the brand, competitors, service or product, category, as well as anything you can think of that will produce an insight or truth about the brand, entity, or audience.

Social (media) listening is the process of collecting candid comments, information, and data about a topic or product/service/company/individual/ cause from social platforms or forums. You then analyze the collected info/ data to find a useful insight.

You could be seeking information or opinions about a brand or a social cause or a habit—anything that will help you understand the who and why. Why is the audience saying certain things? Is there any foundation to what they're saying? To their perceptions? Why do they prefer the competition? What do they think is wrong with the brand? What do they think is spot-on about the brand? What do they appreciate? What do they think about themselves?

Social media listening can make you rethink your approach to advertising or branding (or even the product itself). Domino's® listened to negative customer feedback in a campaign they called Pizza Turnaround. They acknowledged the customer feedback and reinvented their pizza "from the crust up." According to Randall & Reilly, this included extensive media coverage, advertising spots in every major market, documentaries, promotions, taste tests, and national research.

Look at it from the customer's point of view (POV). Become the customer and see it from their viewpoints. Read customer comments and reviews wherever you can. Don't assume the customer's or consumer's point of view or needs.

Ask:

How can you meet the target audience's needs or needs unmet by
    competitors?
What value can you add?

Really get to know the brand community:

What are the brand's customers doing?
What will they be doing next?

Understand the "why" of the audience's behaviors:

What are their pain points, barriers?
What motivates them?
What kind of problem could the brand or entity solve that it has not yet?

> **The task is ... not so much to see what no one has yet seen;
> but to think what nobody has yet thought, about that which
> everybody sees.**
> **—Erwin Schrödinger (1933 Nobel Prize in Physics)**

An Insight

A consumer *insight* is a revelation (an eye-opener) or realization (awareness) about the target audience's need or belief, or the true nature of how
they think, feel, or behave—a truth or finding no one has yet noticed
brought to light. That insight or truth ultimately should warrant respon-
siveness—a change in the way you look at a behavior, situation, branded
product, or service—and it should be the catalyst for idea generation.
For example, Dove®'s Real Beauty Campaign, which has been running
effectively in various iterations for almost 20 years, utilized an insight
first pointed out by women on the team and later confirmed by extensive
research—that "only two percent of women worldwide considered themselves beautiful."

You can think of consumer insights in two main ways: 1) a *fixed insight* that
dominates what the brand says and how it behaves over an extended period

of time, or 2) a *dynamic insight* that bends with micro or macro changes in the audience's needs, situation (think a black swan event, such as a pandemic), or behavior, which is more flexible than a fixed insight.

"I don't want to roll around in what gave us success last year or the year before. I'm appreciative of what got us here, but everything we've done is a daisy chain to the next opportunity," said David Droga at the Future of StoryTelling conference.

A "sweet spot"—the most effective place to hit the audience with your marketing messages—is where creative thinking comes in to make an insight resonate: a functional or emotional benefit that the product, service, entity, or cause offers + an observation about people's needs and aspirations.

Idea Generation

An *advertising idea* or branding or design concept is the creative reasoning—the intention—underlying advertising or brand communication. The idea drives all decisions about copy, art direction, brand voice, and design—what is written or said, how designers and art directors visualize and design, why they select typefaces and select or create images, and the reasoning behind their color palette selections. In advertising, the creative team communicates the idea through the cooperative combination of words (copy) and art (images) and how they art direct and design them. In brand identity design or promotional design, the design concept is communicated through a combination of words and images as well as how they are designed, as in Figure 3.1 where the design concept was to communicate Parle Agro's size and boldness.

An idea can change the way people think about a brand, entity, cause, issue, or individual. It can offer proof, create desire, or stir an emotion that imprints the message. An idea can ignite a conversation, stoke a movement, reframe a conversation, accomplish a social good, press a cultural button, jump on a pop culture moment, taunt a competitor, empower or motivate, endear the audience, or simply amuse.

Generating ideas is an act of discovery and synthesis. Before any creative team starts concepting, they must understand the brief, as I noted earlier, and fully answer the following questions.

Figure 3.1 Branding, Digital: Parle Agro
Studio: Sagmeister & Walsh
Creative Director: Jessica Walsh
Lead Design: Felipe Rocha
Website Design: Felipe Rocha, Gabriela Namie, Julià Roig Fernandez
Additional 3D: João Lucas Gonçalo
3D Animation: Adam Ferris
Client: Parle Agro
"Parle Agro has been a pioneer, creating bold and innovative products and iconic brands since 1985. Headquartered in Mumbai, Parle Agro is India's largest beverage company ... We developed a custom logo font for Parle Agro inspired by the shape of fruit leaves and beverage droplets. ... For Parle Agro, the goal of this branding was to create a unique mark that would communicate their size and boldness in the category. The colors for the branding were chosen to work with the sub-brand colors of all Parle's beverages. In addition to the branding, we developed a full website for them."—Sagmeister & Walsh

Audience Research Tool

Who is the target audience? Answering these questions helps construct a framework for strategic and creative thinking.

- What do they do?
- What's their experience?
- What influences their experience?
- What's their context for the brand or entity?
- What are their needs?
- What issue does the brand or entity solve for them?
- What would they consider an effective solution? An outstanding solution?
- What do they stand to gain from using this product or service?
- What do they think?
- What's their feedback? Concerns? Suggestions for the brand?
- What works for them? What doesn't?
- What do they feel or think about the brand and what do we prefer they feel or think?

Cultural Brand Theory, as pioneered by Doug Holt, has tried to teach us that really iconic brands—the Disneys and Apples and Jack Daniels and Patagonias—do a lot more than teach people about the "attributes" of a product: they cumulatively construct a kind of mythology around a brand that deeply keys into the surrounding culture, a culture that may vary dramatically among consumer groups even in the same country. But we also know that people have multiple goals, like wanting to live close to work but also having enough space for their families, that can conflict. The most successful brands key into our longer-term, hazier goals, for example, not just to lose ten pounds by New Year's, but to lead a healthier lifestyle. The brands and ad campaigns that really have legs and stand for decades align with how consumers see themselves, what they aspire to be, or believe will provide better lives for those around them.
—Fred M. Feinberg, PhD, Handleman Professor and Area Chair, Marketing, Ross School of Business and Professor of Statistics, Department of Statistics, University of Michigan

What Drives People

People respond to advertising and brand design because they want what it's offering: a better lifestyle, self-improvement, delicious food, odor-free armpits, a cooler home, more fun, and so on. People often think: *What's in it for me?*

American psychologist Abraham Maslow's theory of human motivation proposes that five core needs form the basis for human motivation. Maslow arranged the five needs into a pyramid, with physiological needs (air, water, food, sleep, etc.) at the bottom, followed by security needs (safety, stability), social needs (need for love, belonging), ego needs (the need for self-esteem, recognition), and finally at the pinnacle—self-actualization needs (the need for development, creativity).

What Do People Want?

Will your idea address one of the following for people?

- Respond to a desire or wish fulfillment: a yearning, a craving, an inclination. For instance, would wearing a brand of fragrance make someone more attractive? Satisfy a hope with the promise of a positive outcome?
- Address a need, whether emotional or practical, real or imagined. Or point to a need people didn't even realize they had yet?
- Solve a problem with the functional benefit of a product or service. For instance, a brand of cough medicine would help me get through my workday.
- Resolve a pain point.
- Provide fun or entertainment: make someone feel something, cry, say "Aw," be surprised, inspired, shocked, laugh, or think it's so entertaining that they'll share it.
- Provide information or education.
- Provide a utility—a game (think the KFC® "Pocket Franchise" app in China, where a mobile game put fans in charge of their own virtual KFC store via WeChat®).
- Advocate. Allows you to be a standup citizen or identify with a just cause.

Idea-Generation Process

Although people have their own methods and ideation processes, many professionals follow an idea-generation process entirely or loosely based on Graham Wallas's *The Art of Thought* (1926). Wallas, a British political scientist and psychologist, outlined a four-stage model for idea generation: Preparation → Incubation → Illumination → Verification.

In 1940, James Webb Young, a copywriter at J. Walter Thompson, wrote *A Technique for Producing Ideas*, in which he proposed a process for producing ideas based on Wallas's model. I'm going to add a step! Also, I suggest you check out my proprietary ideation method for conceiving worthwhile ideas in my book, *The New Art of Ideas: Unlock Your Creative Potential*.

Step 1: Preparation
Once you define the goal or problem, you gather information. Research with an eye towards discovering an insight. Stay open to any enlightening bit that points to a solution you hadn't anticipated.

Step 2: Initial Ideation (added step)
Analyze, synthesize, and evaluate the data and information. Start to ideate. An insight into the audience is the ideation launchpad.

Step 3: Incubation Period
Get away from directly working on idea generation. Wallas referred to this as a stage when a person is "not consciously thinking about the problem." Taking a break for an incubation period usually allows for *fresher* thinking.

Draw upon your understanding of contemporary culture and your audience, the creative brief strategy, the brand, competitors, and your sensibilities. Think of drawing inspiration from the arts or doodling (semiconscious behaviors, such as doodling, foster incubation). You're not thinking about the problem directly; however, your mind is still turning it over (somewhere in there).

I added Step 2 because for many the incubation process comes after they generate a first-round of ideas directly following Step 1. Then, allowing for incubation, they generate a second-round of hopefully fresher or more focused ideas.

As Jennifer Vandersteen, Design Director, Adjunct Professor, Kean University, advises,

> Business leaders need to create an environment where the creative process can take root. To get brave new ideas, businesses need to be brave new workplaces trusting in their people and the process of perfecting an idea.

Step 4: Illumination and Idea Generation

In an interview with *Big Think*, George Lois, a creative director, agency owner, author, and graphic designer, said that creativity is the act of discovery.[5] The idea should be discoverable. "Once you understand the problem, the answer is there, floating by—you have to grab it," Lois said.

Generating several substantially different ideas is best practice. Variations on one idea won't go far if the person making the final decision doesn't appreciate the core idea.

Step 5: Verification: Crystallizing the Idea

Once you generate an idea, you need to assess it for its strategic creativity.

Critique:

- Does the idea have a benefit?
- Does it address people's aspirations or need for fulfillment?
- Is the core idea fresh?
- Is the idea in accord with the brand's larger narrative?
- Would people engage with it or share it?

Observation

Creative people observe. Whether it's noticing how shadows fall or how someone eats pizza. *Everything is content.* And we all know content is king. Drawing upon observations of the natural world, built environment, human behaviors, and life experiences may be the richest techniques for finding ideas.

Michelle Buteau, Trevor Noah, and Jerry Seinfeld base their relatable observational humor on everyday occurrences. Ideas can stem from how people do what they do—how we eat a sandwich cookie, how we wear glasses on our heads, or how we tug at our underwear. The audience's response should be something like: "Yes, that's how it is. You know me!"

Pop Culture Moments

Is there a pop culture moment the brand can co-opt? This type of solution must happen quickly to stay current. The TikTok newsroom explains how a TikTok creator can inspire a brand:

> A vibe might be hard to define, but the TikTok community knows one when they see one. On TikTok, one creator's vibe can inspire a resonant moment across pop culture, spreading from the TikTok community to the rest of the Internet and IRL world. Enter Nathan Apodaca, a long time TikTok creator using the handle @420doggface208. Combining the unlikely ingredients of skateboarding, cranberry juice, and the classic jam "Dreams" by Fleetwood Mac, Nathan's "morning vibe" took the internet by storm, growing into a heart-warming moment and changing his life forever.[6]

When Apodaca's car broke down on the way to work, he hopped on his board. He recorded his skateboard commute for TikTok, took swigs of cran-raspberry juice from an Ocean Spray® bottle, and sang along to Fleetwood Mac's song, "Dreams." The TikTok video went viral and jumped to other social platforms. Different creators, from Jimmy Fallon to the Ocean Spray CEO, made tribute videos.

Ocean Spray reached out to Apodaca and gave a new cran-raspberry-colored truck to him to replace the one that had broken down the day he made the original TikTok video. Apodaca even became the face of a national TikTok TV commercial that aired during the NBA Finals.

Overstate

BBDO's goal was to make Snickers® relevant again with a global campaign. To do that they returned to a product truth: "Hunger satisfaction." Gianfranco Arena, Executive Creative Director, BBDO New York, and his team landed on the idea that when you're hungry, your personality changes—you might become short-tempered, others might become light-headed or loopy. They used celebrities, such as Aretha Franklin and Betty White, to represent the alter egos of hungry people, using larger than life people to exaggerate how hunger affects people's moods and the satisfaction of eating a Snickers. The now long-running "You're Not You When You're Hungry" campaign is very effective. Global agencies around the world did bespoke versions of the campaign, working with BBDO. "The idea is so relevant to so many people in so many different situations that it makes it incredibly flexible. We can all identify with moments where hunger has caused us to be off our game," explained James Miller, Executive Vice President, Mars Global Head of Planning, BBDO.

Consumers even created their own versions of the idea.

Exaggeration can be humorous as well as memorable. Start with a grain of truth; then, stretch it to a ridiculous extreme.

Facts or Data

When you bring facts or data to life—visually, as an installation, with music, any surprising way—people might respond. This is where data or good research can be very helpful.

For the Illinois Council Against Handgun Violence, FCB Chicago, FCBX, and Lord + Thomas created the "Most Dangerous Street," a walk-through, week-by-week visualization of Chicago's gun violence on one street. Emotional audio recordings of victims' family members telling their stories and laser beams representing each victim of gun violence all greatly affected people and prompted them to take action through a mobile site dedicated to the SAFE Act, legislation needed to obtain funding for economic development in neighborhoods most affected by gun violence.

Remember ...

- Think: Is the idea empathetic?
- Try thinking about a multisensory experience.
- Make it optimistic and kind.
- Think of ways humor disarms people with exaggeration or the unexpected.
- Ask questions—some dissenting, some challenging.
- Combine unrelated things, such as potholes and pizza.
- Can a weakness become a unique selling point or asset? Remember DDB's work for Volkswagen®'s Beetle® in the 1950s and 1960s, for example, "It's ugly but it gets you there."

Everyone can have an idea. As Ana Paola Noriega Cid, CCO of FCB México, quips, "To think we don't have ideas, is an idea." This chapter guides you to recognize strategically creative ones.

Interview with ROSS CHOWLES, Professor of Practice at Michigan State University

Figure 3.2 Ross Chowles, Professor of Practice, Michigan State University
Photographer: Ravi Gajjar

Ross's artistic skills landed him a job as a junior Art Director in advertising in 1980. In 1994, Ross co-founded The Jupiter Drawing Room in Cape Town, Africa's most awarded independent agency. Over the years, The Jupiter Drawing Room won awards in all the major award shows. Ross has had the privilege of judging all over the globe, from Canada to South Korea, including judging The One Show and Cannes Lions. In 2015, Ross was appointed to the international board of The One Club for Creativity. The real skill that Ross picked up in advertising is the ability to understand people and how to motivate them. This manifested in his teaching, both to his staff and his students. Since 2003, Ross has participated every year in The One Show's China student workshop. In 2017, he was appointed to The One Club's main board with the portfolio of education. In 2016, Ross left the industry to become a professor of practice in Michigan State University's Department of Advertising and Public Relations, where he teaches branding, the creative process, and how to create commercial video and ideation techniques. He loves his new job.

What are your five tenets for managing creative people?

It's a simple premise: The better you manage creative people, the better the work they will produce for you. Passion is free. It doesn't cost more to have people passionate for your business. If they love working for you, they'll put in 150% effort. If they hate working for you, they'll avoid your projects or put in the minimum.

1.   Work out what you actually want.

Business is messy. Often clients don't know what they want till they see it. Clients may keep moving the goal posts. These are toxic and abusive situations. What ends up happening is creatives start second guessing you. That situation leads to sub-standard solutions.

The more time you spend defining *what success looks like* for the project, the higher the chance that the solution offered to you will be the right one.

Not only is it important to share *what does success look like* to the agency, but you need to share it with the executive level of your own company. This way there is alignment with the business objectives, and it is also easier to sell the work back into the business.

2.   Inspire them.

How can you expect people around you to be excited about your brand/ product if you are not excited? Marketing is about exploiting potential. The team needs to be able to find that potential. The more you *inspire* them about the product/brand, the more the team around you will be able to find that magic sweet spot. Legend has it that there was a CMO of an adventure clothing and equipment brand. This CMO placed the brief in a box, then placed the box on the slopes of a mountain, and then gave the coordinates to the agency. This is a perfect example of inspiring the creatives about the brand. When I heard this story, the possibilities started igniting in my mind.

3.   Keep the consumer in the room.

In all your discussions with the creatives, your comments should always be framed with the consumer in mind. This keeps the team focused on the objective and removes the "personal opinion" issue. I once had a client who hated beards even though beards were fashionable. This kind of situation steers the attention away from the right solutions for the consumer.

Bringing the consumer into the room will help you when giving feedback on the project.

4.   Spend time talking about the idea.

A typical scenario is: The agency presents work. Then they immediately wait for a response from the client. This is the worst way to run a project.

It puts everyone in the room under the wrong pressure. Bad decisions are made this way.

A better way is to walk away after the work has been presented. Spend some time letting the presentation percolate in your team. This gives you the time and space to explore all the possibilities and negatives without added expectation pressure.

Once you've let the presentation percolate, go back to the agency and spend an hour discussing the idea with the creatives. Discuss the subtleties. Discuss the negative reactions (with social media, there will always be a negative response).

Make sure that everyone, including the creatives who created the idea, understand *what the idea really is*.

Again, bring the consumer into the discussion. Now you can decide to accept or reject the proposal.

The more the entire team understands what the idea is, the higher the chance of success.

This process may seem time expensive, but it will save you time later in the process.

5. Protect the idea from the "business."

Most companies are full of people who place a mark in an Excel® spreadsheet. The company executives are extremely comfortable with making decisions off information on Excel spreadsheets.

However, marketing is dealing with humans. It's magical. It doesn't really fit the Excel spreadsheet world.

Trying to get the rest of the business behind marketing campaigns is very difficult. Fear drives people to make "safe" decisions. *Safe equals mediocrity.*

1. Make sure your agency gives you enough rationale to sell the idea into your business.
2. You then must fend off the onslaught. If you understand the idea and why it will work, it will be easier to defend it. Again, bring the consumer into the room. The business may not like the consumer, but they do understand that they need the consumer.

Creative people are in awe of CMOs who protect ideas.

Those CMOs are highly respected, and creatives fall over themselves to work for them.

What are three points you wish business professionals (business owners, CEOs, clients, marketing teams) understood about the creative side of advertising, branding, and/or graphic design? Please explain.

Clients should know ONE THING and that is **commercial communication** (advertising or design ideas) **done well is unbelievably powerful**.

Great ideas, well executed, can change the fortunes of brands and companies. Just think of what the Volvo's "The Epic Split" ad did for Volvo Trucks.

Clients need to seek out the **best people** in the business, then let them do the job well.

How can people who are not trained in the visual arts best understand what makes for an effective design, branding, or advertising solution? How can you foster an appreciation of art direction in someone who is not a visual artist?

Neither the designer's nor the client's personal taste level is relevant.

The **strategy/brand positioning/personality** should define the taste level.

Is the brand elegant? Then agree on a mood board of elegance—colors, typefaces, photographic styles.

Is the brand brash and bold? Then agree on a mood board of brash and bold colors, typefaces, and photographic styles.

As an industry, we do not spend enough time defining/manifesting the brand's image. If we did this more, clients would understand the taste levels.

What's the value of a fresh idea?

If your idea is normal/average/invisible, then it will be ignored. If it was ignored, the team wasted time and money.

A fresh idea or execution has a higher chance of being seen and noticed. It's that simple.

Any advice on how not to kill a creative idea?

When presented with an idea, fear drives people to look for why it can't work. This is human nature. We are driven by fear to make the wrong decisions.

Rather, spend time exploring reasons why it *can* work.

This exploration will help confirm the brief.

If you still can't see the positive, then you can kill the idea.

Do you have advice on how to discuss creative solutions productively and diplomatically?

This is the key to everything! If everyone involved (client and agency) realize that we are all EQUAL slaves to the objective/outcome of the brief, it gives everyone permission to discuss the project openly and honestly as well as to question everything from the client's brief to creative choices.

As soon as we cloud our behavior with hierarchy, all is lost. Then your actions are not in the best interest of achieving the correct outcome.

Openness and honesty do not mean being rude. There is no place for bad manners in the world.

How can business people and clients avoid the most cautious (or pedestrian) choices? And why?

What I've learned is that clients and creative people fear ridicule more than anything. They are so scared to be **that** person who messed up. (Just think of the Pepsi® protest TV commercial.)

The problem with marketing is it's so visible and everybody can see the public response. That fear now means that the industry makes bland choices. Bland choices will mean the marketing becomes ineffective. Which in turn means money was wasted because the goals were not achieved.

To achieve the marketing goals, you absolutely must be provocative and attract the attention of the agreed consumer. Remember, the modern consumer is suffering from attention deficit syndrome as well as breaking under information overload. An invisible brand campaign just ain't gonna cut it.

The campaign must be bold and provocative. If it is provocative, this means a portion of the population will complain on social media. How you deal with this negativity is by exploring what could be the possible negative reaction before you launch. Then the business needs to sign off on that possible negative reaction.

What are key issues about cooperation, collaboration, inclusion, and diversity for business and creative professionals to keep top of mind?

Collaboration and cooperation *are* the tickets to the game. If you are not collaborating with people, then you're not in the game. With Zoom and technology, we can collaborate with anybody!

The old-style agency was kind of limited by the staff that it had. Whereas the new agency can collaborate with the best typographer in Japan or use a writer who is very good at a specific style of writing but lives in Argentina. This kind of structure is much more exciting and dynamic. However, the caveat of collaboration is you need **one person to be the leader**. You need one person to make the calls and take responsibility.

Diversity is the very nectar of creativity. If you are all the same, you all talk the same, and you all look the same, you are going nowhere. We live in a stunningly diverse world, and for creativity it's an essential ingredient. Diversity in races, cultures, genders, the arts, foods, etc.

Diversity makes for interesting and alive creative thinking.

How can companies and brands build trust and authentically become allies?

You build trust walking the talk.

You build trust by sticking to "it" year in year out.

The problem with marketers and brands is they dip in and dip out of whatever is the flavor of the month. That kind of behavior lacks any sincerity.

The "issues" should be relevant to their product or their target consumer. Also, they must commit to it with money or action. Better, commit with both.

The brand must **walk the talk**. It's that simple. A brand or company can't say one thing and do another. Consumers aren't fools.

Please talk a bit about appropriation.

There are two types of appropriation. The first kind of appropriation is when we draw from society or from arts. A Marvel®-style comic or a Wes Anderson-style commercial. I think this is perfectly acceptable. The second is when we borrow from a culture that has specifically been historically oppressed or abused. I think this is unacceptable.

But appropriation leads into a bigger issue. That issue is that brands tend to create marketing that is a mirror to the consumer, so they keep on just showing the consumer rather than creating a personality built around their own brand.

If a brand spent all its money defining its own personality and not using someone else's personality, the consumer would know the brand.

Red Bull® does this best. If you look at all the Red Bull communication, it's not about the consumer, it's about Red Bull and their "vibe."

Ninety percent of commercials just show the consumer. What that does is it makes the brand bland. It makes the brand personality look like the consumer rather than the brand having its own distinctive personality.

Of course, if a brand's provenance is relevant to its proposition, then appropriation would seem natural. For example, if the brand is Japanese and there is something in Japanese culture that elevates the brand in the minds of the consumer, then use it, by all means.

On representations of power: How can people become more sensitive to how identities are represented or marginalized?

This is such a complex area. The first premise is that everybody is damaged, and so it doesn't matter what you do, somebody will be upset. Somebody is feeling misrepresented or not heard.

The second premise is that *one person* can't speak on behalf of a community. Marketers often make this mistake. "There was a woman in the room" is not research. It's not being sensitive to people.

What do you wish clients and business people understood about being a creative director (or a creative professional)?

Business lives in a world of spreadsheets and facts. Where whether they are dealing with distribution, production, rentals, or whatever, all those examples can be put on a spreadsheet and business loves that.

Marketing is magic and magic is elusive. The business world hates elusive. Thus, the business world looks down at this magic. Now add the word "creative," and the kind of image that business conjures up is people with pink hair and piercings through the nose. Instantly trust or respect is lost.

Yet the truth is that marketing/advertising/creativity well done is **extremely** powerful. In fact, in a world of parity, it's the most powerful tool that any brand or company can have.

Apple® doesn't always have the latest or fastest technology. Yet through a great design ethic and "think different" image, their products are the most expensive (higher margin) and they are one of the world's most valuable companies.

Take the Audi TT. That design totally changed the look of Audi and the fortunes of the business. Before the TT came along, Audi had a boring design style. It was the boring version of the three German luxury brands. Now they are in a totally different position and creativity got them there.

Business must stop thinking that creativity and creative people are not to be taken seriously. Creativity is innovation and innovation = surviving the future.

However, I need to say that a few creative people sabotage our rightful place around the boardroom table by acting like insensitive, selfish children.

Notes

1   "Les Binet and Peter Field Discuss Brand Marketing in the Age of Hyper-targeted Messaging," *Think with Google*. January 21, 2021. https://www.youtube.com/watch?v=82k1jnhcwmY.
2   Tim Nudd, "Fernando Machado on the Making of 'Moldy Whopper,' Burger King's Craziest Ads Yet," *Muse by Clio*, accessed July 4, 2021. https://musebycl.io/advertising/fernando-machado-making-moldy-whopper-burger-kings-craziest-ads-yet.
3   Bella DePaulo, "9 Ways the Most Boring People Will Bore You," *Psychology Today*, accessed July 4, 2021. https://www.psychologytoday.com/us/blog/living-single/201409/9-ways-the-most-boring-people-will-bore-you.
4   Gabriel Schmitt, "The Strategy Behind Burger King's Whopper Detour Campaign," *Contagious*, accessed July 4, 2021. https://www.contagious.com/news-and-views/burger-king-whopper-detour-strategy-cannes-interview.
5   "Big Think Interview with George Lois," *Big Think*. April 5, 2010. https://bigthink.com/videos/big-think-interview-with-george-lois.
6   "Doggface gives the world a smile with juice, a skateboard, and all the vibes," *TikTok*. October 14, 2020. https://newsroom.tiktok.com/en-us/doggface-gives-the-world-a-smile-with-juice-a-skateboard-and-all-the-vibes.

There is a reason storytellers are revered and salesmen are reviled. No one likes to be pitched. It feels icky. Great copywriting makes a sale without feeling like it's making a sale. It's insightful, it has personality, it entertains, it makes you feel something. Rather than writing a sales pitch, think about how or why your product is relevant to your consumer, then tell that story.

—*Rachel Abrams, Copywriter/Creative Director and Brand Storyteller*

Chapter 4

Strategically Creative Copywriting

Thinking Like a Copywriter

In case you're thinking, *I'm not a writer*, don't worry, because you are.

If you can converse with friends and colleagues or explain how to do something, such as wash your hands or cook pasta, then you can write. When you write, you are essentially communicating something to someone else.

For some folks, writing sounds so formal that they freeze. If you think of writing like chatting—recording the spoken word—it is less intimidating and easier to accomplish. In fact, most effective advertising copy sounds conversational (unless it's aimed at a specific trade audience, such as physicians or engineers, for instance, where it may well be more technical).

The point of thinking like a copywriter is to become better skilled at getting a message across by grabbing and keeping people's attention. Thinking like a copywriter also builds the soft skill of empathy. Understanding what your audience thinks or feels and what they want not only makes for a good writer, it makes for a darn good friend, romantic partner, or colleague.

The most important point is this—you'll be able to evaluate copy when you read it and make informed suggestions or offer an informed critique about its efficacy. You may already have that ability; however, this content will turn it into a super strength. Ultimately, thinking like a copywriter leads to strategic creativity.

To think like a copywriter, keep these three objectives in mind: 1) Grab someone's attention with fresh phrases or sentences, 2) Communicate a clear takeaway message to the right people, and 3) Gauge the copy from the audience's perspective. The reader should think: "Oh yeah, that's so true!" or "You know me."

Copy that Isn't (Obviously) Selling You Something

In a 24/7 entertaining, wired world, it's a challenge to grab people's attention. If we classify copy in one of two categories—sales pitch and not a sales pitch—it immediately acts as a weed cutter. Copy should sound fresh.

DOI: 10.4324/9781003230786-4

Sales pitch: Your ticket to becoming a millionaire.
Not a sales pitch: "Hey, you never know." (New York Lottery)
Sales pitch: Run With the Best!
Not a sales pitch: "Just do it." (Nike)
Sales pitch: Milk Tastes Great!
Not a sales pitch: "Got milk?" (California Milk Processor Board)
Sales pitch: 15% Off. Get it now.
Not a sales pitch: "15 minutes could save you 15%" (GEICO®)

Contrived phrases with superlatives often sound like sales pitches. Conversational phrases and sentences, something you would naturally utter in a friendly conversation, far less so. Conversational and interesting headlines and taglines not only grab your attention, but they are more likely to keep attention.

Communicating a Clear Takeaway Message

If I'm trying to be clever, I might forget the takeaway. However, if I think outright, *What am I actually trying to say?*, then I can ensure the takeaway message.

> **Clear thinking leads to clear writing. If you don't really know what you think or what you're really trying to communicate, you'll never say it clearly. Many of us write to figure out what we think. That's great. But once you've figured it out, you have to go back and edit so you're clear the whole time. That's the difference between professional writing and a journal entry.**
> **—Leigh Muzslay Browne, Creative Director, GSD&M**

The takeaway message may not be direct. For example, "Got milk?" implies that milk is a good accompaniment to food. That question, written so informally, also makes you hear someone say it aloud. It makes you think you're taking part in a conversation at the kitchen table.

"Hey, you never know," doesn't literally tell you to purchase a New York Lottery ticket, but it does make you think you have a chance to win if you do buy one. Using the word "Hey" helps set the casual tone, as if someone is speaking directly to you, again in conversation.

Lead with Empathy—Look at Everything from the Audience's Pain Points

In advertising, branding, or graphic design, you're always seeking an insight into what makes people tick—the people you're communicating to. That means you take their needs, desires, interests, and values into account. For example, would a sassy voice offend the people you're aiming at? Or would a sassy voice be more likely to ignite a conversation with them? You also take the zeitgeist (what's in the cultural air) into account—or you create the cultural air.

Can you utilize slang authentically? Would it sound organic or fake?

Does the voice or tone jive with the brand or entity's values and actions?

What are your audience's desires and goals? Pain points? What keeps those people up at night?

Igniting conversation is what makes a brand social.

The Strategically Creative Copy and Image Relationship

What is fairly unique about advertising is the frequent, fundamental cooperative/synergistic relationship between words and images. Few other forms of writing have a similar relationship—with the exception of children's picture books, where the singular line of text must complement the illustration. If a picture book illustration depicts a child giving a bone to a big red dog, then it would be a very dull book indeed if the text accompanying that illustration read, "A child is giving a bone to a big red dog." Not the makings of a page-turner.

The ad idea drives the nature of the relationship between image and copy. Image and copy cooperatively communicate the ad idea. Approach the copy/image relationship by determining which one will be tasked with the heavy lifting—dominate to communicate the message—and which one will provide support or contextualizing.

There are two basic guidelines when conceiving and structuring headline/image relationships:

1. You hear the word *synergy* a lot. Well, here it totally applies. Working synergistically, the headline and main image communicate more together than either could alone. Cover the headline and look at the image. Cover the image and read the headline. Either alone isn't communicating as much as the two together—in a thoughtful ad, that is.

2. The headline and main image should *not* be redundant. If you show a horse, then don't write or say "horse."

Ways to think about and assess copy/image relationships across media channels:

- Either the headline or image is the point of focus, drawing the viewer's attention first; they should not compete to be the focal point, though they always work in concert.
- Conceive a straight man/wiseacre relationship: if either the headline or the image is straightforward, then the other is clever or funny. In a comedic pairing, the "straight man" is the one who says the things that allow their partner to make quips or wisecracks. Some refer to this as a straight/crooked relationship. If both the headline and image are straightforward, the ad might be boring. If both are clever, they might fight for attention. Bottom line: if the image is the attention-getter—it is odd, humorous, shocking, or interesting—then the copy should be straightforward or direct. If the copy is the attention-getter, then the image should be direct. Like a classic comedy team, this relationship always is synergic.
- Contrast headline and image for an ironic effect, if appropriate. You could think of this as a surprising relationship as well. For example, the ad might imitate a greeting card, where we see a common winter holiday image of people exchanging gifts, except the copy and image contrast—the image is typically pleasant, while the copy is a selfish ode.
- As always, think of the people who you're aiming at. Would they prefer images or copy? If it's copy, are the words compelling enough to grab and keep their attention? Again, is it addressing what keeps them up at night or entertains them?

Quickstart Guide to Writing

A copywriter's job is to communicate with an audience to illuminate, seduce, cajole, promote, inform, or educate. A copywriter is a conceptual thinker who can generate ideas and work to communicate them through a combination of words, words + images, or words + images + sound + movement, depending upon the media channel.

Business professionals, leaders, and owners communicate daily through emails, reports, case studies, press releases, and other written endeavors.

Now let's work on how to write copy and understand how it best works in advertising and communication design.

Intent

Once the team has digested the creative brief and, ideally, summarized the brief in a one-sentence goal and reviewed the research, the writer ideates with their partner, the art director (or whoever else might be a team member). The idea and brand drive the purpose, voice/style, passion, and content of the copy. What does the written or spoken word in the advertising set out to do? And why should anyone care? Strategically creative copy has a purpose:

- *Seduce*: Grab attention.
- *Compel*: Through persuasion or cajoling, convince people that this brand, entity, issue, person, or cause is worthy of their time, attention, or money.
- *Inform*: Raise awareness, generate interest, or educate people about what the brand, entity, individual, issue, or cause is and what benefits it offers—what it can do for people. And keep the brand, entity, or cause alive in the audience's mind.
- *Create desire*: Meet people's needs and wants. Keep in mind that many branded products and services subtly or overtly promise transformation (healthier hair, heightened athletic prowess) as well as sensation (refreshment, cool air, or bursts of flavor). How does the ad copy respond to the target audience's needs or foster desire?
- *Create community*: Connect like-minded people. Get people on board with the brand and brew their desire to belong to the brand community. Get people thinking, participating, engaging, and talking. Turn people into brand sirens.
- *Reinforce identity*: People use brands as shorthand for representing their ideal selves—in other words, they are the type of person who would own this or eat this or drive this.
- *Tell a story*: Each ad tells a very short story and a longer one over time. People are drawn to stories with distinctive voices and styles.

Copy must grab attention, be well written enough or engaging enough to sustain the reader's interest, as well as add value to the message. To accomplish this, you tap into what people really want, into their behaviors and psyches, and direct that desire towards the brand, entity, or cause. And write well.

Writing: Tips on Mechanics

1. *Write short sentences.* Start with a subject plus a verb. For example, "He throws the ball." Or, "She dances to country music." Cut unnecessary words. Contemporary writer John Grisham agrees. In his list of "Do's and Don'ts for Writing," he advises, "Do—Read each sentence at least three times in search of words to cut."[1]

2. *Use the active voice and action verbs.* The active voice makes it clear who is performing the action. The subject directly performs the action.
   Active: The boy kicked the ball. (Here, we know who is kicking the ball.)
   Passive: The ball was kicked. (Here, we don't know who kicked it, which is not direct enough for advertising or communication design.)

> **Copywriting is problem solving, just like any other job. The only difference is that our tools are words. Ask how creative thinking and words can solve the business problem. After that, say it the simplest and most interesting way you can, but with the comfort of knowing your copy has resilience in the face of small tweaks. Something that can't be said of simple wordplay.**
>
> **—Thomas Kemeny, Creative Director/ Author of Junior**

3. *Keep the writing lean.* In *On Writing*, Stephen King advises this. Avoid the use of adjectives, especially language that has become synonymous with advertising hyperbole, such as, great, best, better, amazing, and so on. Some writers avoid adverbs too. For lean writing that delivers a punch, read fiction-writer Raymond Carver's work, historian Simon Schama's nonfiction, or columnist Gail Collins's pieces in the *New York Times*.

4. *Avoid cliches, well-worn phrases, and jargon.* Write conversationally, as if you're speaking to someone. Copy shouldn't sound like a sales pitch, canned, or trite.

5. *Don't use a thesaurus.* Well, I take that back. At times, looking up a word in the thesaurus helps you find a better, more exact word, but it shouldn't be the wrong word or the most impressive word. For example, if you look up contemplate, you might find the word "ruminate" listed as a synonym. It's not an accurate synonym. To ruminate means to chew the cud, staying stuck on the same thought over and over.

6. *Write short paragraphs*. Due to digital media, people have become accustomed to reading content in chunks or short bits of information at a time. Unless the copy is for a longer form, such as branded entertainment, keep it pithy and focused.

7. *Write for the target audience*. Address the target audience only, *not everyone*. Know your audience, their culture, and cultural communities. Engage with your target audience's interests and people's lifestyles, e.g., sports, art, entertainment, or food. Keep in mind that slang or vernacular might be acceptable for certain audiences. For example, dog lovers might use invented terms or words, such as "good boi" or "doggo." It's always contextual.

8. *Allow the reader to think for themselves*. If you spoon feed, people won't experience the small joy of decoding the message. (But don't be opaque or cryptic, either.)

9. *Pair copy/image in a complementary way*. If the copy will be coupled with an image of a blue hedgehog, don't write "blue" or "hedgehog." Keep the reader engaged by not repeating. I've said this before, so you know I mean it.

10. *Ask yourself: Does the copy make sense?*

Rhetorical Strategies

In advertising, rhetorical strategies are often used to help illustrate a point of difference. It's good to be able to recognize some of them:

- *Compare and contrast* cites the similarities and differences of two or more things: ideas, things, brands, places, etc.
- *Cause and effect* is used to help people understand why something happened or what could happen. For example, if you don't sign with a good insurance company, you won't have the protection you need when you get into a car accident.
- *Explaining a process* to make it accessible is a strategy that describes how something is done, from waxing a hardwood surface to baking lasagna to using a remote to back up your car.
- *Defining* involves telling the audience what something means, which might include examples.

- *Describing* is a strategy that involves providing the audience details about a person, place, thing, or issue, which might include how something tastes, smells, feels, or sounds.
- *Narrating* is telling a story.

Writing: Tips on Expression

How you construct your sentences or phrases will affect expression and, of course, the reader. Copy that delivers a gut punch or tickle is more memorable. Here are basic guidelines:

1. *Begin with the end goal.* The seed of the written content is in your responses to these two questions: What's the brand promise in this ad? What should the reader's takeaway be?

2. *Every ad tells a story, even if it's a short one.* What is the story about? *Who is telling the story?* Whose voice is it? The brand's or company's voice? Spokesperson? Brand character? A mother? A doctor? Someone we see in the ad? A disembodied voice? In any ad or marketing copy, the copy takes on a voice.

3. *Make room to surprise yourself.* This is how many creative professionals work. Although some delineate outlines and know what will happen at the outset, others allow for a creative adventure. In an interview in *The Atlantic,* Andre Dubus, an American writer, told Joe Fassler that he loves this line from E.L. Doctorow: "Writing a novel is like driving at night. You can only see as far as your headlights."[2] Dubus continued,

   > but you keep going until you get there. I've learned over the years to just report back anything that I see in front of the headlights: ... What's on the side of the road? ... What's the weather? What are the sounds? If I capture the experience all along the way, the structure starts to reveal itself. My guiding force and principle for shaping the story is to just follow the headlights. That's how the architecture is revealed.

4. *It's how you tell it.* Thousands of people can tell the same story or joke. It will always be different. What you leave in. What you cut. The tone. The pace. Rhythm. Say it aloud as you write. Listen for the flow and rhythm.

5. *Let your unconscious write.* Writing is a rational process; however, it is also informed by the unconscious. Affording your unconscious mind a significant role is how creative professionals work—it's the crux of creativity. *Work without self-consciousness.*

6. *Show. Don't tell.* Anton Chekhov said, "Don't tell me the moon is shining; show me the glint of light on broken glass." Advertising is about proving things to people and providing reasons to believe what we're saying. When you *tell* people, you're asking them to believe you without evidence. If you allow the audience to *witness* the characteristics, qualities, or evidence of the benefits of a product, service, cause, or company, then they can come to their own conclusions. *Showing* is substantiation. For example, instead of writing, "Mike is tall," you could write, "When he was sleeping, Mike's feet hung over the edge of the bed."

7. *Say it directly, in plain language.* To start, write it the way you would say it to a friend. Keep it clear and based on the central concept and message. It's especially important to make the writing accessible if the target audience's first language is not the one you're writing in and if the copy might be translated.

8. *Remember the brand promise.* Tout the benefit, not the product or service. If you focus on the "why" behind the brand's or cause's promise—the reason to believe—you'll be on track.

9. *Be trustworthy.* US President Harry Truman said, "Say what you mean, mean what you say. Keep your word."

10. *Find a distinctive voice.* Differentiate from the competition, otherwise your copy just advertises for the category, rather than the specific brand or entity, or for a competing brand. Voice, tone, and style all should reflect that specific brand's values and attributes, not your own style. (People appreciate distinctive voices, whether it's a sound or a writing style—just think of Robyn Rihanna Fenty's or Joy Williams's style.)

11. *Make it relatable.* People will identify with the communication if they can relate. Observe people. Practice social listening. Find out what people are saying, thinking, and commenting on. Investigate what ignites conversations on Twitter®.

12. *Take a positive stance.* Ernest Hemingway learned this tip from his days as a reporter for the *Kansas City Star.* Write what something is rather than what something isn't (unless you're doing it for effect).

13. *Write like a person,* not like AI or a catalog of facts.

14. *Respect your audience*. If it makes sense for your brand or idea, the writing can be brazen or satirical, but it should *never* be disrespectful. Be inclusive.

Copy Critique Rubric

When critiquing other people's work, be diplomatic and kind. Lead with empathy.

To assess if copy is effective and engaging:

- *Analyze*: Examine how the language and usage convey meaning. Look at how the overall purpose, intent, and message are communicated. Is there a key takeaway? If the copy is coupled with an image, is the relationship cooperative?
- *Stickiness*: Determine if the audience would find it engaging or shareworthy. Is the messaging on target for the audience? Would it affect people on an emotional level?
- *Assess*: Does it add value? Make good on the brand promise?
- *Freshness*: Copy should sound fresh, not stale or like a sales pitch.

> If you're trying to persuade people to do something or buy something, it seems to me you should use their language, the language they use every day, the language in which they think. We try to write in the vernacular.
>
> —*David Ogilvy*

Exercises: Start Writing

Write concisely. Delete what can be deleted while still retaining meaning.

Your Bio

Write your bio in three sentences:

First line: Establish your credibility with your credentials.
Second line: Explain the problem you solve.

Last line: Make a personal connection—something about yourself that will connect with people, such as, write about your German Shepherd or growing tomatoes on your terrace.

Twitter

Twitter affords conversations between brands, entities, individuals (think politicians, celebs, prominent citizens), and the Twittersphere audience. Its 280-character limit promotes brevity. Plus, you can pack meaning into a hashtag.

1. Select an issue that is meaningful to you, such as protecting the environment, reducing waste, healthcare, or homelessness.

2. In 280 characters or less, write your point of view on the subject. Be conversational.

3. Think: Would like-minded people retweet this? Is it shareworthy? Would it ignite a conversation?

Taglines

A *tagline* or *strapline* is the catchphrase that communicates the brand's essence and position in the marketplace as well as conveys the brand or entity's strategy for a campaign or a series of campaigns.

1. Select a favorite brand that doesn't have a great tagline.

2. Select an appropriate tone of voice for the brand, for example, snarky, cheeky, witty, punny (think "Don't stand for hemorrhoids" [Preparation H®]), silly (think "Taste the Rainbow" [Skittles®]), explanatory (think "Buzzed driving is drunk driving" [US Department of Transportation], or aspirational (think "The best a man can get" [Gillette®]).

"Ain't No Party"

"Coolio started it," writes David A. Graham in *The Atlantic*,

The ubiquity of the "ain't no party" phrase is matched only by its promiscuity. In any situation—party or not, endless or not—it's a favorite crutch for television writers and creators of cyberephemera alike. How did a phrase from a mid-'90s rap hit become a signal formula in the Internet age? It's a tale of appropriation, but it's also a story of how old culture is recycled and rescued from obscurity in unlikely ways.[3]

How would you utilize this phrase yet make it fresh?

Exercises: Keep Writing

To improve your writing for the sport of it:

Exercise 1: In writing, explain how to boil an egg or hit a golf ball.
Exercise 2: Write an Instagram® poem about your love of a particular food.
Exercise 3: Write zany descriptions of objects, such as one of a garbage pail.
Exercise 4: Respond to the following writing prompt: *Little did they know …*
Exercise 5: Write your own birth announcement.
Exercise 6: Scroll through Twitter. Write a reply to a brand's tweet. Keep it positive.

Remember poet and novelist Robert Graves's point: "There is no such thing as good writing. Only good rewriting."

Interview with NICK SONDERUP, Executive Creative Director at Pereira O'Dell

Figure 4.1 Nick Sonderup
Photographer: Kevin Hatt
(http://www.kevinhatt.com)

Nick Sonderup is the Executive Creative Director at Pereira O'Dell in New York City, leading creative across all accounts. Throughout his career, Nick has spent time at a number of creative shops, including Wieden + Kennedy, BBDO, MTV®, Translation, and Ogilvy & Mather. He has worked on global and iconic brands such as MINI®, Stella Artois® (Figure 4.2), General Electric® (Figure 4.3), American Express®, ESPN® (Figure 4.4), Nike, AT&T®, Corona®, Starbucks®, State Farm®, MTV, the American Red Cross, and more. Nick's work has been recognized in nearly every advertising and marketing awards show and publication, including the Emmys®, Cannes, AICP, Clio Awards, Andy Awards, Effie Awards, The One Show, Art Directors Club, *Communication Arts*, BDA/Promax, Epica, CMYK, and more.

Nick directed and produced a film titled *100 Bands in 100 Days* that premiered at the 2009 SXSW® film festival and screened at many more festivals globally. Nick was also the Creative Director and Co-Producer of the Woodstock Comedy Festival (2013–2018), a three-day festival in Upstate New York, working with iconic comedic talent like Gilbert Gottfried, Colin Quinn, Robert Klein, and Jim Gaffigan, among others. Nick has also contributed writing and photography to music and sports publications. He is a passionate music lover, concertgoer, and road cyclist. Nick lives in Brooklyn with his wife and twin daughters and spends most of his free time pedaling on two wheels or cooking in a tiny kitchen.

What should business people understand about writing for different media?

Different media have different needs and rules. The term "rules" should be used loosely here, since in advertising the rules are meant to be broken. But one rule can't be broken—your message needs to be tailored to the medium in which it's being consumed. Of course, an advertising campaign is most effective when it communicates one very simple message. Then, that message needs to be tailored across the media landscape to fit the readers' need for that medium.

There may be a temptation to just apply the same messaging whatever the media, but the danger of that approach is that you won't meet the audience where they are or acknowledge how they respond to that medium. For example, TV audiences want to be entertained and expect inspiring storytelling. They're already settled in to be entertained, so the goal of that medium is to be as memorable as possible: simple, broad, easy to remember, and inspiring. This is a medium for dramatic storytelling.

In print, out-of-home, and social media, the goal is still to entertain and inform; however, the message needs to be much quicker, tighter, and more concise. The goal is to leave the reader with one simple message, but you have much less time, so you have to be sharp.

One thing to always remember: Nobody wants to see your ad. It doesn't matter what media form it comes in, people actively try to avoid it. So, tailoring your message to the medium, and how the audience behaves and responds to that medium, makes all the difference. You're competing for their attention.

What should everyone involved understand about hopping on cultural moments? About co-opting pop culture?

Co-opting pop culture is often one of the best ways for a brand to experience a real earned media moment that can get more attention than traditional media or a whole original creative concept. But if it comes across as borrowed interest or opportunistic, it can backfire.

Similarly, attempting to hop onto cultural moments is a tricky proposition that needs to be handled with great care. The risk and reward can be huge. The risk is making the moment too much about your brand and not enough about the moment. This path can backfire and leave your brand looking selfish and shallow. For example, just posting a black square during the "Black Lives Matter" movement may have seemed like a message of solidarity, but it was generally thought to backfire and leave the brand looking like an empty promise of solidarity, particularly if the brand made no real commitment to addressing the issues behind that movement.

On the flip side, when done right, though, the reward is that it can make a brand a hero of the cultural moment and leave the audience not just satisfied but wanting more. A great example of hopping on a wave was when, moments after a power outage during the Super Bowl, Oreo® tweeted: "Power outage? No problem. You can still dunk in the dark." This was a great example of hopping on a cultural moment that millions of Americans were experiencing together and making it better.

Please offer tips on creative collaboration.

The best creative collaborations come down to one simple rule: Hire great people and let them do the thing they are great at. When it comes to a creative partner, this is key. If you want great TV commercials, hire a world-class agency that produces TV commercials. If data solutions are what you seek, hire an agency that specializes in data.

But that's only step one. Once you've hired that partner, then the real collaboration begins. One of the most valuable parts of the

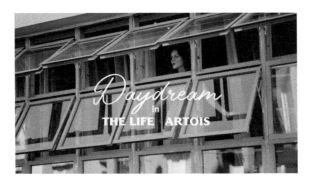

Figure 4.2 Stella Artois "Daydream (In the Life Artois)"
Client: AB InBev, Stella Artois US
Vice President, Stella Artois: Lara Krug
Communications Lead, Stella Artois: Lauren Denowitz
Media Lead, Stella Artois: Ralph Conserva
Digital Lead, Stella Artois: Katherine Gruneisen
Public Relations Director, Stella Artois: Laura Alito
Agency: Pereira O'Dell
Creative Chairman, Co-Founder: PJ Pereira
Chief Creative Officer: Robert Lambrechts
Executive Creative Director: Nick Sonderup
Creative Director: Thiago Cruz
Senior Copywriter: Ivan Rivera
Senior Art Director: Camilo Ruano
Copywriter: Anjali Rao
Art Director: Rachel McEuen
Associate Design Director: Som Perry
Production Artist: Evan Zelermyer

creative-collaboration process is knowing how to give feedback on a creative idea. How do you do it? First, tell your creative partner the issue, not the solution. Say what you're not getting from the idea, not how to get it. Let them come back to you with a solution that takes your notes into consideration. Step number one to gaining trust in a creative collaboration is knowing that the receiver of your notes has the opportunity to solve the problem. Because they want to solve it.

The hardest thing to do in collaboration is to let go, but it's also the most important. You don't have to figure it out yourself. You don't need to have all the answers. Instead of saying, "Let's do it my way," think "Let's do it *our* way."

Figure 4.3 General Electric "Childlike Imagination"
Agency: BBDO NY
Chief Creative Officer, Worldwide: David Lubars
Chief Creative Officer, New York: Greg Hahn
EVP/Executive Creative Director: Eric Cosper
EVP/Executive Creative Director: Michael Aimette
Creative Director/Copywriter: Nick Sonderup
Creative Director/Art Director: Eric Goldstein
Director: Dante Ariola

Figure 4.4 ESPN "World Cup Murals"
Agency: Wieden + Kennedy NY
Executive Creative Director: Kevin Proudfoot
Executive Creative Director: Todd Waterbury
Creative Director: John Parker
Creative Director: Stuart Jennings
Copywriter: Nick Sonderup
Art Director: Eric Stevens
Art Director: Mathieu Zarbatany
Illustration: AM I Collective

One very powerful thing you can say, which is often the hardest thing to say during creative collaboration, is "I don't know." This opens the door. You're no longer purporting to have all the answers. You're not throwing up your hands and giving up. You're actually creating an opening.

What makes a brand iconic?

Guts and timing. Simple as that. The guts to be bold. The timing to be relevant. Oh, and money. It sounds simplistic, but iconic brands are playing the long game. They invest because they know a brand doesn't become iconic overnight.

What do you wish clients and business people understood about your job?

Creativity takes time. It's one of the most crucial elements of the process. We move so fast these days, and no one allows for it. We don't need a month, but we do need more than 48 hours. Not because we want to play ping pong, but because we want to plant the seed and then help it grow.

Notes

1   John Grisham, "John Grisham's Do's and Don'ts for Writing Popular Fiction," *New York Times*. May 31, 2017.
2   Joe Fassler, "The Case for Writing a Story Before Knowing How it Ends," *The Atlantic*. October 8, 2013. https://www.theatlantic.com/entertainment/archive/2013/10/the-case-for-writing-a-story-before-knowing-how-it-ends/280387.
3   David A. Graham. "'Ain't No Party': Examining the Origins of a Ubiquitous Phrase," *The Atlantic*. February 11, 2015.

Good design is good business. Typography is a key element in good design. It is a powerful design tool that can influence others, inspire action, and create change.

Typography is more than custom letterforms or the selection of a typeface to represent the brand. The effective use of type—from hierarchy to alignment to measure—affects readability, informs navigation, aids in retention, and delivers the message with clarity and interest.

—*Kristin Leu, Principal, Leu Design*

Chapter

Strategically Creative Design

Seeing Like a Designer

Let's imagine you're on vacation in a quaint town, and you stop to browse in the local bookshop. You've no book in mind. A display of books is in the center of the sales floor, big and appealing. You walk over to a table filled with new hardcover books by local authors and quickly scan the display. Even though you are not familiar with the author's work, you pick up a book. Why did you select that book? I'd bet my daughter's college fund that the efficacy of the cover design had something to do with it.

Designers use shape, form, color, texture, patterns, images, and typography to attract your attention, communicate messages, enhance meaning, and produce impact.

Now you're in a supermarket. Again, you're browsing. Perhaps you'd like to try a new flavor or different brand of tea or coffee. What makes your hand move towards one package and not the other, even if the flavors are the same? A high percentage of decisions about packaged goods are made in front of the supermarket shelf. Package design influences purchases. Effective design influences people.

Just What *Is* Brand or Graphic Design?

Brand and graphic design are visual communication. They are visual representations of ideas relying on the creation, selection, and organization of visual elements—type and images. A logo. Brand identity. Branding program. Wayfinding system. Book cover. Poster. Magazine cover and interior. Annual report. Corporate communications. Website. An app. An Instagram post. Movie title. Twitter background. Banner. Package design. Album cover. And more. A design solution can brand, identify, inform, locate, rouse, engage, and convey meaning. Using type and images, design:

- Makes information and content accessible.
- Represents a brand or entity's essence, identifies it, and imprints it.
- Builds brand communities and brand advocates.
- Makes useful brand apps, websites, experiences, and platforms.
- Can be tangible, digital, experiential, or hybrid.

DOI: 10.4324/9781003230786-5

- Can be solutions that benefit society, not just selling more branded products and services.
- Is social media campaigning that maps back to the brand proposition and narrative.

Looking at Design Through the Lens of its Underlying Structure

To better appreciate and evaluate effective branding, art direction, and design, examine any work through the lens of its underlying structure—how the designer or art director utilizes the graphic elements and components of design as well as how they use design principles to arrange elements into a composition that attracts people.

To communicate with people, you first must capture their attention. Well-designed compositions, arresting imagery, and well-crafted typography capture people's attention across media channels. To keep people's attention, the composition must give *coherent and impactful form* to the content.

Become Familiar with the Principles of Design

Remember that book you picked up? Someone purposely selected the imagery and typeface. They arranged all the component parts so that you would find the book cover's form interesting. Breaking down what we see provides greater understanding of the principles of design.

Composition is the form, the whole spatial property and structure, resulting from the arrangement of graphic components (type and images) in relation to both one another and the format (boundary edges and shape of the screen, page, or other substrate). Designers and art directors use formal elements (line, shape, color, value, and texture) to visualize imagery and type, employing basic compositional principles (balance, emphasis, unity, rhythm, and proportion) in the process of composing and creating graphic space.

Balance

In visual communication solutions (works that intend to communicate to a mass audience), balance is a must. Otherwise, viewers might have an uneasy response or perhaps even be repelled.

Balance refers to the stability created by an even distribution of visual weight on each side of a central vertical axis, as well as by an even distribution of weight among all the elements of the composition. Employing symmetry and asymmetry are two main ways to balance a composition.

Symmetry refers to the mirroring of equivalent elements, an equal distribution of visual weights on either side of a central axis (see Figure 5.1).

Asymmetry refers to the balancing of one weight with a counterweight to achieve an equal distribution of visual weights without mirroring elements on either side of a central axis (see Figure 5.2).

Arranging an asymmetrical composition requires judging the visual weight of colors, shapes, forms, textures, patterns, and their relative size, position, and relationship to their neighbors in the composition. Elements are weighed against one another to ensure balance. For example, by balancing one element with the weight of a counterpointing element, designers Scott Laserow and Natalia Delgado balanced the composition of the *Making Posters* book cover (Figure 5.2) without mirroring elements on either side of a central axis.

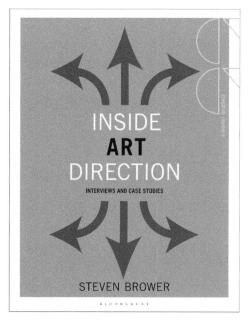

Figure 5.1 Book Cover: *Inside Art Direction: Interviews and Case Studies*
Art Director/Designer/Author: Steven Brower
Publisher: Fairchild/Bloomsbury
The title, sub-title, arrows, author's name, and publisher are all centered on a central vertical axis with a mirrored distribution of visual weight on either side of the axis. This cover design is almost symmetric; it is an example of "approximate symmetry," rather than symmetry, because the imprint logo in the upper right-hand corner is not mirrored on the left.

Figure 5.2 Book Cover: *Making Posters*
Authors/Designers: Scott Laserow and Natalia Delgado
Publisher: Bloomsbury Visual Arts
"In the last chapter of *Making Posters*, we discuss emerging technologies like animation and augmented reality (AR) and how they influence the way posters are being created and consumed. When designing the cover, we wanted to highlight this technological evolution while paying homage to the medium's origins. Our solution was to create a visual representing a wall with a series of wheat-pasted street posters wrapped around from the front to the back of the book. To add some mystery, we kept the posters blank until they came alive through AR using the free Artivive® smartphone app, playing as a looped animation. This feature allowed us to showcase many posters included inside the book without being limited by the constraints of the printed surface while making a playful connection with our audience simultaneously."
—Scott Laserow and Natalia Delgado

To check for balance, visualize a vertical axis and see if one side of the composition (one side of the axis) appears visually heavier than the other.

Visual Hierarchy

To guide how a viewer's eye scans a composition, you must rank images and copy in order of importance, emphasizing and organizing content from the most important to the least important. For instance, if you want to order the information on a business card, it's unlikely that you'd want the zip code to take prominence.

There are different ways to achieve visual hierarchy, from simple to complex. Visual hierarchy cues the viewer.

"Look here first.
Now look here.
Then look here."
And so on.

What do you want people to look at first: the image, headline, title, or brand name? By arranging graphic elements, you attempt to guide a person's gaze through a composition. Since people do not spend more than a few seconds glancing at an ad, logo, or book cover, designers use the principle of visual hierarchy to facilitate communication and guide a person's eye scan. *Emphasis* is the arrangement of visual elements according to importance, stressing some elements over others or making some graphic elements dominant and others subordinate.

Since most of us are accustomed to reading a page from the top down, that's the simplest way to create a visual hierarchy. To get people to look at a position that is not at the top of the "page" (poster, mobile ad, website, any format), you need to attract viewers' eyes to look somewhere else first, for instance with bright or saturated colors, odd shapes, the size of the graphic component, movement in the case of motion design, bold patterns, or textures. The size of a graphic component—a big image or large-sized typography—can call attention. When an element attracts the most attention to itself, we call it the *focal point*—the part of the design that is most emphasized, as in Figure 5.3. You create a focal point within a visual hierarchy by emphasizing one component and de-emphasizing others.

Scale also comes into play—the size of an element or form seen in relation to other elements or forms within the composition. If all of the shapes in an ad are big except for one small one, you might be attracted to the small one first. It all depends upon how the designer utilizes scale.

If the designer or art director doesn't guide the viewer's eye scan, it can be challenging to communicate a message quickly. People might stare at a painting or drawing for a long time, but they won't give more than a couple of seconds to an ad or logo unless it's directing their gaze to communicate the message or meaning. To be memorable, the composition must hang together—be unified.

To judge visual hierarchy, ask yourself: What do I see first? Second? Third? Is the designer guiding your eye scan well enough for you to understand the communication?

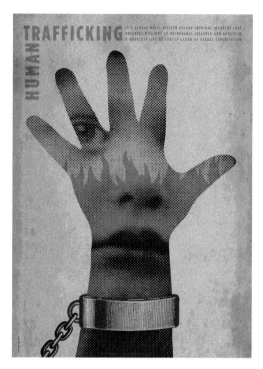

Figure 5.3 Poster: "Human Trafficking"
Designers: Joe Scorsone and Alice Drueding

Unity

Unity occurs when all elements within a composition appear to be harmonious and belong together, forming a cohesive unit. To achieve unity, a designer or art director utilizes design principles to produce *correspondence*, a visual relationship among the components that creates a sense of belonging via color, style of imagery, typefaces, characteristics of shapes and forms, the use of light and dark, textures, patterns, and so on. For example, if red is repeated a few times throughout a design solution, it likely contributes to establishing unity.

Any entire branding program, campaign, website, or single design solution must look unified. The principle of unity is about producing cohesion. To establish a correspondence of component parts throughout a branding program, series, campaign, or composition, there must be sufficient repetition of graphic elements (color selection [palette], textures, patterns, type of imagery, typeface) to create unity yet enough variety to create some visual contrast, which makes a work more interesting (Figure 5.4).

Figure 5.4 Book Cover Series: Penguin's Georges Simenon Novels
Author: Georges Simenon
Art Director: Jim Stoddart
Designer: Jamie Keenan, Keenan Design
Publisher: Penguin
Jamie Keenan creates visual variety from cover to cover in this series yet maintains a series look and resemblance.

We all want logos to be memorable. Unity plays a huge role in making all of the elements in a logo hang together and appear as a cohesive unit. The same goes for a package design, brochure, or any brand touchpoint. Think of unity like a song—a composer wants the entire piece to work together as a whole unit.

To check for unity, ask yourself: Does all of the imagery, typography, and graphic elements hang together or act in concert to create a sense of wholeness in a single composition or throughout a program, series, or campaign?

Rhythm and Flow

To get people to scan the entire composition, a designer must create rhythm, a visual beat, a design principle for single or multiple pages, screens, and motion graphics. *Rhythm* is a pattern created by repeating or varying elements; the space between elements also contributes to a sense of movement from one element to another. Rhythm helps guide the viewer's gaze through the compositional graphic space. It's comparable to a beat in music.

Rhythm is critical to establishing a coherent visual flow from one graphic component to the next on a single surface and/or from page to page. A designer also must employ *flow*, the arrangement of elements in a design so that the viewer's eyes are led through the design from one graphic component to another (see Figure 5.5). Where you position elements in the graphic space and the intervals or interstices between and among them are key to promoting flow from one to the other.

The *arrangement* is how the designer or art director structures the positioning of graphic elements and components in a composition.

Figure 5.5 Book Cover: *A Shock*
Author: Keith Ridgway
Art Director: Erik Rieselbach
Designer: Jamie Keenan, Keenan Design
Publisher: New Directions
Our eye scan flows easily from one letter in the title to another.

To check for flow, think of the composition as a highway—there should be no road barriers to the flow of traffic.

Graphic Space

Whether you prefer a landscape or a still life, when you look at a painting of either, you're admiring the pictorial space (the illusion of three-dimensional space) created by the artist on the surface of the canvas, paper, or screen. In graphic design, we call the space that results from the arrangement of images and type on a two-dimensional surface—digital or print or in motion—*graphic space.*

A *transition* is a spatial interval between graphic elements in a composition or between the elements and negative space that enables one's gaze to migrate from one graphic element or movement to another. Spatial intervals and transitions contribute to rhythm and flow. By focusing on the transitions and interstices—those *spaces between* shapes, forms, and type—the entire composition will appear organically interconnected.

Illusion of Spatial Depth

To create the illusion of spatial depth on a two-dimensional surface, designers manipulate graphic elements. They must be aware of the surface called the *picture plane*, which starts out as the front plane of a page or screen. For example, Jamie Keenan creates an illusion of graphic space in his cover design for *A Shock* by putting a cast shadow behind each letter in the title, which helps to create layers of spatial depth (see Figure 5.5).

Using Western conventions for graphically depicting three-dimensional objects and spatial relationships on two-dimensional surfaces, many designers describe the illusion of spatial depth in terms of three major planes: the *foreground*, which is the part of a composition that appears nearest the viewer; the *middle ground*, an intermediate position between the foreground and the background; and the *background*, which is the part of a composition that appears to be in the distance or behind the most important part (see Figure 5.6).

In contemporary Western art, some artists and designers create the illusion of volume and space by loosely utilizing the linear perspectival system developed during the Italian Renaissance, which is based on the observation that as objects recede in space away from the viewer they appear to get smaller or parallel lines and planes appear to converge to distant vanishing points, mirroring how we see.

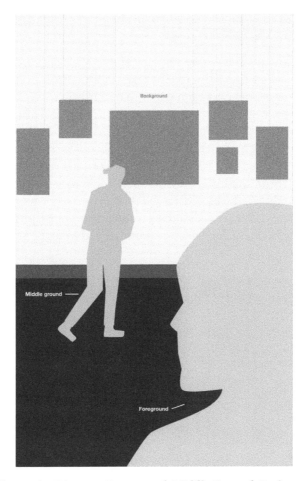

Figure 5.6 Illustrative Diagram: Foreground, Middle Ground, Background
Illustrator: Mara Reyes

To assess the illusion of spatial depth, ask yourself: Does any element (color, object, word, image) appear to look as though it is in front of another?

Figure/Ground Shape Relationships

Is that a white cat on a blue background?

When looking at a design or any visual art, your mind first seeks to discern what it perceives as figures, then it moves on to what it perceives as the ground (or background) elements. Is that a tree? Is that a vase or two people's profiles? We tend to seek what we can easily identify, which is usually pictorial. People seek cues to distinguish shapes representing figures from those comprising the (back)ground.

Figure/ground shape relationships, also referred to as *positive and negative graphic space*, are a basic principle of visual perception that refers to the relationship shapes have to each other, particularly the relationship of a figure to the (back)ground, on any print or digital two-dimensional surface. The *figure* or *positive shape* is a definite shape, whether it's pictorial (think flower, fish, shoe), as in Figure 5.7, abstract (somewhat removed from what we see but still recognizable as a person, creature, or thing), nonobjective (think triangle, cube, trapezoid, brushstroke, any shape or form that doesn't conform to what we recognize in the world), or letterforms. The shapes or areas created between and among figures are known as the *ground* or *negative shapes*. Considered negative shapes can also create visual interest.

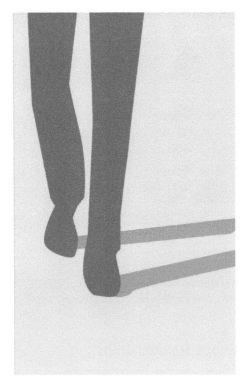

Figure 5.7 Diagram: Figure/Ground Shape Relationship: "Walking Man"
Illustrator: Mara Reyes
Photo Source: Danielle Garcia

When judging a design, check to see that negative graphic spaces also create pas-
sageways—promoting flow and movement through the composition and around
shapes and forms. Do negative graphic spaces contribute to rhythm? Do they help
direct the viewer's gaze?

Composition Evaluation Checklist

- Is the composition balanced? Does there seem to be an equal amount of visual weight on either side of an imaginary vertical axis that divides the format in half?
- Is there a clear visual hierarchy (images and copy arranged in order of importance)?
- Is either the image or copy the focal point?
- Is the composition unified? Do all of the graphic components (type, imagery, color, and other elements) have a visual relationship?
- Does the arrangement of the components and elements move your eyes through the graphic space with ease? Does one element flow to the next?
- Are the transitions among the graphic components interesting? Have you considered all of the negative space and all of the transitions among graphic components?
- Is some amount of contrast used to create visual interest?

Typography Basics

Each typeface has a visual voice. As Canadian poet and typographer Robert Bringhurst explains, "Typography is the craft of endowing human language with a durable visual form."[1]

The visual voice of the typeface is the emotional tone, which is expressed by the particular characteristics of the specific letterforms (and type classification), for example, ITC Bodoni has a warm voice, as if crafted by an artisan; Univers has a neutral, spare voice; Mrs Eaves has a polite voice; and Bungee has a playful voice.

Each letterform is made up of positive and negative shapes. The strokes of the letterform are the positive shapes (also called forms), and the open spatial areas created and shaped by the letterform are the negative shapes (or counterforms).

To appreciate the design of a typeface, look at the shape of the letterforms, the inherent balance in the design of each letter of the alphabet, the proportions, the axis, the characteristics of the letterforms' shapes (shape of the letter) and the open spaces (counterforms), and the detailing (shape of the serifs or lack of serifs).

To give voice to ideas, designers and art directors consider the following when selecting an appropriate typeface:

- Whether a suitable typeface best expresses the design concept.
- Type and image integration (how the specific visual characteristics of the typeface and image will cooperate).
- The visual voice of the typeface, e.g., loud, sweet, rude, witty, conservative, edgy.
- Legibility and readability (how easy or hard it is to make out the letterforms and read the typeface on paper, on other substrates, or on different screen sizes).

> **The selection of type is critical and cannot be left to novices. When commissioning or evaluating typographic work, always consult with a design professional with a sensitivity to or specialty in typography.**
> **—Liz DeLuna, Professor, Graphic Design, St. John's University**

- Whether there is sufficient value contrast between the typeface and the background.
- Context: Whether it will be read in print or on screen (or both), what the size will be, and whether they will be dealing with small, medium, or large amounts of text.
- How letter, word, and line spacing contributes to typography (poor spacing detracts from message communication and speed of reading).
- Its suitability for the audience, design concept, message, purpose, and context.
- The typeface's appropriateness to brand voice and essence.
- Whether it pairs well with/complements the brand's identity and typeface.

Exercise: Learning to Examine Typefaces

Take note of the *counter* of the uppercase O—the enclosed or partially enclosed area within the character. Is it perfectly round? Oval? Do the counters and counterforms of the typeface integrate well with the characteristics of accompanying imagery?

Notice the counter shapes of a typeface to help judge the aesthetics of the forms.

To judge typographic design quality, notice the spacing between the letters and words and lines of type—does the spacing slow down or enhance reading? Is the typography integrated with the images? Is the connotative meaning (suggested meaning) related to the denotative (direct) meaning?

Pairing Type/Image Checklist

When you critique design solutions that pair type and images, use this checklist. To best communicate the message, consider:

- Should the typeface share visual characteristics with the image?
- Should the typeface contrast with the characteristics of the image?
- Should the typeface be neutral (not draw attention to itself) and allow the image to drive the solution?
- Should the typeface dominate the solution? Should the typeface carry the main communication and the image be subordinate to it?
- Should the typeface be eminently readable?

Interview with GAIL ANDERSON, Designer, Writer, and Educator

Figure 5.8 Gail Anderson
Photographer: Nir Arieli

Gail Anderson is the Chair of BFA Design and BFA Advertising at the School of Visual Arts (SVA) and the Creative Director of the Visual Arts Press at SVA. Anderson serves on the Citizens' Stamp Advisory Committee for the United States Postal Service and on the advisory board for Poster House, the New York City poster museum. She is the recipient of the Cooper Hewitt National Design Award for Lifetime Achievement and is an AIGA Lifetime Achievement Award medalist. Anderson is co-author of 15 books on design, typography, and illustration, and her work is in the collections of the Library of Congress, the National Museum of African American History and Culture, and the Milton Glaser Design Archives at the School of Visual Arts.

What are five points you wish business professionals (business owners, CEOs, clients, marketing teams) understood about the creative side of branding and graphic design? Please explain.

I'd love for business professionals to understand that we're on your side—our job is to help you succeed. The best designers are not in it for the accolades and "likes," though those are lovely occasional bonuses. We love strategic thinking and are trying to look at your business from

360 degrees. We're about more than just making something cool or trendy or whatever your preconceived notion about designers is.

I'd also ask for trust in our creative expertise. We don't mean to dismiss what your friends, children, or life partners think, and we do want to work collaboratively. But we really do hope you'll have faith in our judgement and desire to sometimes push you outside your creative comfort zone.

How can all of us in this industry work towards ensuring diversity, equity, and inclusion? What do business people, clients, and creatives need to do/know?

You just have to start—easier said than done, of course, but it comes down to making a commitment. We need to invest in the next generation of BIPOC creative professionals, which in some cases could involve funding scholarships, paid internships, or other kinds of professional development. Creative directors need to look beyond ye olde mental Rolodex of friends and colleagues and welcome different kinds of designers into the fold.

The dirty little secret in our industry is that it's harder to find a job as you get older. Design itself sometimes looks like a young person's job (especially as you become an old person!). If you want to be hands-on and not in a creative director or design director role, the perception is that you need to be a groovy kid tethered to social media. We have to carve out places for designers of all ages who have *soooo* much to contribute but are often overlooked ("He'll be too expensive!" "I'd feel weird managing someone so much older than me!" "She's not going to know technology!").

Please offer tips on creative collaboration.

I learned a lot about creative collaboration working with Fred Woodward at *Rolling Stone* so many years ago. I was young. I was a giant sponge, and Fred was a genius, so that was a no-brainer. But my years with Drew Hodges at SpotCo represent both an enlightening and brutal period of growth as a collaborator with clients—a whole different kind of learning process, to say the least. We worked *with* brilliant visionaries, and we worked *for* difficult, high maintenance micromanagers. "With" and "for" are key here. When you're working *with* someone, you're collaborating, even if it's sometimes awkward or possibly a touch adversarial. But you're on the same team. When it devolves into working *for* a client, the joy is slowly sucked out, and you're a pair of hands. The client loses out here, and it's hard to muster up the A work or go the extra mile. Smart clients know this; the others, not so much.

What's the best advice you've ever given to a client?

"Here's this other thing I was playing around with—I know it's a bit different than what we were talking about but let me know what you think."

You've created design solutions for celebrities and esteemed theater folks. Please share some advice on how to get people who are used to getting their way to be open to your ideas.

I learned this from Drew—let the client who's used to getting their way take credit for your idea as if they'd come up with it themself. Be willing to let them own that gem, even if it feels like you're just stroking their ego. It's win-win for all involved, and it's not really about you, anyway. A few weeks or months later, you've all moved on, and you've got a great design and a great story!

I'm only half-kidding here. I learned to be a better listener in my years at SpotCo and to always try what's been suggested, even if the idea sounds absurd. You can't just blow past it—when you really think about it, you wouldn't want someone to ignore *you*, right? Sometimes the client is flat-out right, and it just took you both a while to better understand the problem at hand. And, my toughest lesson—sometimes your seventh sketch is the best one instead of that first idea you thought was pure genius. So many mid-career life lessons learned (or maybe I've just been worn down).

Have an open mind, don't be defensive, and work with your client as a partner. Involve them early in the process and talk about ideas that might not be working quite yet. Transparency makes things so much easier and staves off the assumption that designers just want to make groovy things for themselves.

Interview with ALEXANDER ISLEY, Alexander Isley Inc.

Figure 5.9 Alex Isley, Alexander Isley Inc.

Alexander Isley's distinctive, editorially driven design combines text and imagery in ways that reflect imagination, confidence, spirit, and humor. Alex first gained recognition in the early 1980s as the senior designer at Tibor Kalman's influential studio, M&Co. He went on to serve as art director of the funny and fearless *Spy* magazine. Alex founded his firm in 1988 in New York City, and in 1995 he relocated the office to Connecticut, to work in a barn surrounded by trees.

Alex has created award-winning identity, communication, environmental, interactive, and publication design programs for an unusually wide range of clients.

He holds a degree in Environmental Design from NC State University and a BFA from The Cooper Union in New York. He has taught graphic design, typography, and exhibit design at Cooper Union, RISD, and the School of Visual Arts. For over 15 years, he served as a lecturer and critic in the graduate program of the Yale School of Art.

In 1993 Alex was named an inaugural member of "The *I.D.* 40," a survey of the country's leading design innovators. His work is in the permanent collections of the Museum of Modern Art, the Smithsonian Institution, the Zurich Design Museum, the Poster House Museum, the Letterform Archive, and the Library of Congress.

Alexander Isley is a recipient of the New York Art Directors Club Herb Lubalin Memorial Award for Art Direction and Design, the NEA International Design Education Fellowship, the SEGD Global Design Award, the Webby Award, and the Federal Design Achievement Award. He is past president of AIGA New York and is an AIGA Fellow. In 1998, Alex was elected to membership in AGI (Alliance Graphique Internationale), an international association of designers who represent the highest level of professional achievement.

In a recent *Graphic Design: USA* magazine poll, Alex was named by his peers as one of the most influential designers of the past 50 years.

In 2014, Alex was awarded the profession's highest honor, the AIGA Medal, in recognition of lifetime achievement and contributions to the field.

What are six aspects of the creative side of branding and graphic design you wish business professionals (business owners, CEOs, clients, and marketing teams) understood? Please explain.

1. Before taking on any initiative, a designer first needs a good understanding of the client's organization, what needs to be accomplished (not just what needs to be designed), who the audience is, what they care about, what they need to know, and what misconceptions they might have. Without that knowledge, anything the designer does is just decoration. And if the client does not have all this information, the designer needs to find a way to get it.
2. What something looks like should be the last thing to be decided.
3. There is more than one way to solve a problem.
4. Getting acceptance of a solution often takes longer than developing it.
5. If a client decides to update their look or their logo, a lot of people are not going to like the change. You will need to prepare them to deal with pushback, as it's easier than ever for people to complain in a public way. Pro tip: Tell your clients to tough it out for a few weeks, and the noise will soon dissipate. (Unless you've designed something that is truly terrible, of course.)
6. The first question I ask is, "Why do you want to change your look?" If they can fully and persuasively articulate the need for a change, that's a great start. "We're tired of what we have" is not a good enough reason to make a change.

Your studio puts an enormous amount of effort into thoughtful client presentations. Please tell us why your presentation methodology resonates.

Developing a design solution that works—that addresses a challenge, that connects with a specific audience, that communicates an idea, that solves a problem—is difficult enough. What's even more difficult is convincing a client to accept the idea and invest their emotions (and dollars) in the idea. A lot of what designers do might seem subjective, but it's important for me to convey that every decision we've made along the way has been carefully considered.

When I present our work to clients, the first 50% of a presentation is usually a review (or reframing) of the assignment: What tasks were we given? How did we approach them? Who did we talk to? What did we discover? What did we try that worked and, more important, what did we try that didn't work?

I think a mistake that a lot of designers make is that they make a presentation, show a solution or two, and say, "Well, what do you think?" As the designer, you might have spent two or three weeks struggling with the assignment every single day, whereas the client might not have given it much thought at all since the day you were given the brief.

In my presentations I do a quick recap, reminding everyone what the challenge was, what we learned from our discussions, what we explored, and how we endeavored to solve the problem in a skillful and effective way. This shows that design is a process and, while each challenge is unique, it can be approached in a thoughtful way.

I've found that as the clients join you on this journey, they come to better understand how you've arrived at your decisions, and appreciate that you're not just making something that looks good but, rather, something that actually does something.

Ultimately, I want what we do to seem simple, perfect, and effortless. Like it just naturally happened. A lot of effort goes into making something seem effortless.

You've said, "The person who has the authority to approve a project must be among those who provide the initial input and direction. Otherwise, everyone's in trouble." Please elaborate.

I'll only undertake an assignment if (a) I can meet with the ultimate decision-maker before starting work to get her thoughts, and (b) if that same decision-maker will be present in person for all key presentations. In fact, this is written into our agreements.

It's important to avoid the situation in which we need to present a solution to someone who has to "take it upstairs" for approval. That's the space where messages get muddled, intentions are misunderstood, and nuance (and courage) evaporate.

As a designer, it's important to hear directly from the one who's doing the approving, where you're working together to do something great (instead of being afraid of looking bad if something risky does not work).

There's a special thing that happens when you're having an exchange of ideas with a smart decision-maker. Quite often, you'll come out of a discussion with something extra, a missing piece of the puzzle, or a small spark of an idea that pushes the idea in a new and better direction. This rarely happens when you're talking to someone whose job it is to present your work to the decision-maker. Those exchanges don't happen.

"Good work only happens when there is trust," you've said. Why should clients and other business pros trust their design team?

So much of what we do is subjective: Why did you use that particular word? Why does that shape look the way it does? Why that font?

At some point someone needs to make those calls, and if your client has started to feel comfortable with your thinking and the way you've been making decisions, it's all for the best. It's all about trust.

When I was starting out, I was almost always younger than my clients. I felt that gaining their trust was a real challenge. I remember hoping for the day when I'd have gray hair and wrinkles (meaning that I'd have a track record and body of work that would result in my being more trusted).

I'm now at a point where I have that experience and, I'm happy to report, don't have to fight quite as hard to get people to go along with something unusual or unexpected or seemingly risky. The gray hair and wrinkles? Be careful what you wish for.

You've also said, "A brand is the promise of an experience." Please elaborate.

I've heard lots of definitions of what a brand is.

I believe if a company or organization has a well-articulated brand, and if (big IF) they contribute something that is of value, whenever someone hears their name or sees their logo or something they've produced, they'll get a good feeling.

If everything works together well, the very thought of the organization suggests a rewarding experience.

You believe that "when clients are honest and divulge their budgets upfront, they'll get a better, more resourceful, and more creative solution from their designer. Honest." Please tell us more.

I always ask for a project's budget for a couple of reasons. If the clients really don't have one, it often means they are not experienced or have not thought things through very well. (The other, less common scenario is that they are so well-off that money is no object. That situation has only happened to me once.)

If they act more circumspect and claim they don't have a budget, or they have a budget but won't share it with you, I suspect it often means they think you'll try to take advantage of that information and charge them more than you ordinarily would. That's not starting from a place of trust.

I wish clients would realize that most designers see budget limitations as a challenge, and we'll often over-deliver to overcome such constraints. And if what they've set aside is more than we'd need, I let them know that. Better to save the extra for another project and have both parties come away feeling good.

If you really can't get a sense of a client's budget, I've found it can be helpful to say upfront, "You know, this sounds like a $XX,000.00 project. Is that something you're comfortable with?" If they say yes, you can spend your time putting together a detailed proposal. If they say no, you can have a conversation about adjusting scope and deliverables, or you can just shake hands and move on with best wishes.

You believe that "it's easy to take something that is truly great and, through the power of consensus building, turn it into something good." How can clients and the other business people involved avoid this?

Don't agonize. Don't show things around to everyone hoping for a consensus verdict.

Instead, go with your gut. I find that initial reactions to proposed solutions are usually good, honest, and valuable. This is not to say that ideas can't be refined and polished, but I always look for that first reaction when presenting a design.

At the end of our presentations, I show a card that says:

Next Steps:

- Review Concepts
- Select a Direction to Pursue
- Don't Agonize.

Individuals don't always recognize how their taste is affecting their judgement about a designer's creative solution. How should clients and business people approach and analyze a design solution presented to them?

This is tough, because emotion is involved, and so many decisions relating to design are subjective. I try to explain how we've arrived at what we're showing, and how, while I want us all to feel good about what is selected, the decision needs to be based on more than "I like it" or "I don't like it." (I try not to let anyone get away with saying that, and I always push for more of an explanation.)

The only time I let "I don't like it" slide was when a client said he hated a dusty rose color because it was the color of his mother's dining room, and he hated his mother. I decided to let that one go rather than twist the lid off *that* discussion. It didn't really need to be dusty rose, anyway.

Please offer advice on how to productively and diplomatically discuss creative solutions.

I find that telegraphing my excitement about a solution works wonders. I'm really into what we do, and this attitude seems to come across and is commented upon often. I realize this sounds like a calculating presentation strategy, but really it's not.

When a client doesn't know exactly what they want, what's the best way for them to discuss their objectives with a designer?

I always write a creative brief as a first step when starting a project. Visual solutions are not addressed in this document, but it outlines the project's objectives, issues to address, pitfalls to avoid, and how success will be determined. The client gets to review, amend, and approve this brief.

For selfish reasons, having this in place helps me do a better job and it also serves the role of encouraging the client to articulate what we're trying to achieve in advance of their evaluating any work. This enables the whole endeavor to get off to a good collaborative start.

Figure 5.10 Packaging and Identity Program
Design Firm: Alexander Isley Inc.
Creative Director: Alexander Isley
Designers: Matt Kaskel, Shannon Stolting
Client: Philo Ridge Farm

Figure 5.11 BAM "New Music America" Poster
Design Firm: Alexander Isley Inc.
Creative Director: Alexander Isley
Designer: Alexander Knowlton
Writers: Yale Evelev, Alexander Isley
Client: Brooklyn Academy of Music

Figure 5.12 "Empty Sky" New Jersey 9/11 Memorial
Architects: Schwartz Architects: Frederic Schwartz, Jessica Jamroz
Design Firm: Alexander Isley Inc.
Creative Director: Alexander Isley
Designer: Hayley Capodilupo
Client: The State of New Jersey

Note

1   Robert Bringhurst, *The Elements of Typographic Style*, 3rd ed. Vancouver:
     Hartley & Marks. 2004.

For many creatives, the idea is half the battle. But executing it and bringing it to life with Art Direction... that's what takes a great idea and makes it THE idea. Giving creatives the proper amount of time and resources in this stage is important to avoid rushing a great idea that ends up falling flat in the execution.

—Erin Evon, Associate Creative Director, Saatchi & Saatchi

Chapter

Branding & Art Direction

Thinking Like a Brand Storyteller

As I worked with a student named Sam, I noticed a "Just Do It" sticker blazoned on his laptop case. I asked him about it. Sam is studying advertising; however, that's not why Sam chooses to reference this tagline every time he works.

"Just Do It," inextricably linked with the Nike brand, is a definitive statement of intention. Sam reminds himself to put his shoulder to the wheel and get on with it. "Just Do It" is the narrative to which Sam subscribes.

How does a brand refrain become a mantra? A frame? How does an advertising tagline move from a brand promise to a philosophical belief? You might find the answer in another question: What motivates people and how can you turn their desire or aspiration into a brand story?

To think like a brand storyteller, consider two main aspects of crafting the underlying concept for a brand story that will resonate. First, the brand narrative must align with the brand's values and actions. Sounds like a no-brainer; however, many companies think they can say something but not back it up with actions. Secondly, the brand narrative must align with a driver of human behavior.

Aligning with a Brand's Values and Actions

Most people can sniff out inauthentic brand claims or stories. Many also embrace brands, organizations, and individuals who deliver on their brand promises and do as they claim. If you talk about sustainability, it's best if your company's practices are sustainable. If you talk about empowering women, your company had better employ female top executives and act equitably.

What kind of brand narratives do people find meaningful? Of course, it is contingent upon the specific audience and sector; however, many people respond to brands that:

- Are purpose-driven, motivated by a core mission.
- Give back to their communities or are rooted in their local communities.

DOI: 10.4324/9781003230786-6

- Provide opportunities and brand experiences for fans to come together, whether hybrid, digital, or in person.
- Are sustainable and conscious of our planet, wildlife, water, forests, and so on.
- Treat their employees and supply chain providers (think farmers, growers, etc.) well.
- Contribute supportively to cultural conversations.
- Allow people to participate.
- Are authentic.
- Lend a hand during tough times (think pandemics, natural disasters, wars, etc.).
- Rally round a good cause or issue.
- Consider LGBTQIA+ communities.
- Ensure accessibility.
- Work towards social justice.
- Work to reverse the consequences of systemic industrialization.
- Work to eliminate existing hegemonic systems.

Let's revisit "Just Do It," whose origin story is surprisingly morbid. Dan Wieden, an advertising executive who co-founded the Wieden+Kennedy agency in Portland, Oregon, had an odd source of inspiration for the now ubiquitous tagline. In the documentary film, *Art & Copy*, Wieden said the idea for the line was ignited by the last words of convicted murderer Gary Gilmore, who said, "Let's do it!" to the firing squad just before his execution. The phrase "do it" was the inspiration for Wieden's pitch to Nike.

In 1988 one of the first "Just Do It" ads featured Walt Stack, an 80-year-old marathon runner from San Francisco. Over 30 years later, with the "Dream Crazy" campaign, the "Just Do It" ethos evolved into a social justice message starring Colin Kaepernick, the NFL Super Bowl quarterback. Kaepernick, following his ethical convictions, peacefully protested by kneeling during the national anthem in protest of police brutality and racial injustice on the fields of the National Football League, which ignited both a controversary and national conversation. Kneeling has a history in the Black rights movements. "The kneel has been a kneel about articulating the promise and desire of freedom from oppression," explained Rinaldo Walcott, the Director of the Women and Gender Studies Institute at the University of Toronto, adding that this is what Kaepernick was trying to address.[1]

In one spot, Kaepernick says, "Don't ask if your dreams are crazy. Ask if they're crazy enough." "Believe in something," Kaepernick states, "even if it means sacrificing everything." And he did.

According to the Effie Awards (for marketing effectiveness), the Nike "Dream Crazy" campaign

> showed how the brand's deep belief in the potential of athletes and the power of sport can make an enormous impact on popular culture and in the process drive unprecedented brand relevance and business success. By showing how athletes could not only push themselves in sport, but also begin to change the culture around them, this campaign captivated today's youth generation—and American culture at large.[2]

Align with Drivers of Human Behavior

People want outcomes when they purchase products or services (think whiter teeth, peace of mind as a homeowner, better entertainment, and so on) or they engage with organizations or causes for improved outcomes (better government, safter streets, greater social justice, and so on). The brand story must offer some implicit or explicit benefit focused on people's desired outcomes. Ask: *How does the narrative align with the target audience's drive to actualize or simply live better?*

Major drivers of human behavior:

- Survival: Does it aid subsistence, health, or stamina? Does it promise sustainability for the planet?
- Pleasure: Does the overarching brand narrative offer the potential for enjoyment?
- Safety: Does it provide peace of mind or reduce risk?
- Community: Does it help people get by? Does it nurture a sense of belonging?
- Love and Sex: Does it help people find love or be more loveable? Will it lead to physical pairing?
- Self-esteem: Does it promise improvement or aspiration fulfillment?
- Status: Does it improve someone's standing or help them gain approval? Does it add to someone's prestige?
- Rivalry: Does it offer a competitive advantage?
- Influence: Does it promise power?
- Convenience: Does it save time or energy? Does it eliminate pain points?
- Development: Does it supplement someone's education or expertise?
- Exhilaration: Does it promise thrills or delight?

Brand Construct

Because most products or services in a price category are on a par, brands build constructs to differentiate themselves. A *brand construct* is a theoretical assembly of three main points: 1) what people want and might need in the near future, 2) how the brand fits into what people want as well as anticipate what they might appreciate, and 3) how the brand attributes are portrayed as distinctive in a very crowded commercial arena.

Together with the construct, the branding idea drives the execution. Designers take many different approaches to how they visualize a construct and idea. Nijel Taylor, a design director, explains his philosophy:

> Simplicity is about clarity and truth. By employing simplicity, you unlock a future where you reach more people more effectively and with more impact. Simplicity can transport you to places you never dreamt you could go. The purpose of simplicity is to get you out of your own way to let your ideas shine.

The Brand's Role in People's Lives

A colleague of mine was the executive creative director on a national supermarket brand account. He and his team conceived a TV commercial campaign that angered many mothers across the US, their target audience. His idea was to portray the supermarket as a caregiver. Although each TV commercial in the campaign was beautifully executed, he got the role of the brand dead wrong. The mothers who protested viewed themselves as the caregivers with the supermarket brand as a helper.

A brand can take on a role as long as it makes sense for the brand's values, mission, strategy, positioning, and the people you're aiming at. All aspects of the strategy need to be in sync. A brand or entity's role can morph or even be multifaceted (though that's challenging); however, the role must relate back to the mission, core brand strategy, overall narrative, and performance. Key: as my colleague now will tell you, the role must be aligned with the target market's perception of themselves. Here are some examples of roles:

Alchemist: It will allow you to harness your powers, transforming you into the person you aspire to be (think Pilates, Peace Corps, or continuing education). Metamorphosis—think from 97-pound weakling to strong man.

Catalyst: It will instigate the change you need or desire in your life or in the world (think Inc.com, American Red Cross volunteer program, or Cavendish Pianos).

Coach: It will motivate you, act as your personal trainer (think Nike or Noom®).

Entertainer: It will transport you, make you forget your work or life's woes and offer entertaining content. The brand might even play inside a game with you (think Wendy's®) or give a free game to you (think KFC).

Guardian: It will protect you (think LifeLock®), your health (think GlaxoSmithKline, Pfizer, or BioNTech), your possessions (think Allstate®), wealth (think Fidelity®), and community (think Illinois Council Against Handgun Violence).

Guide: It will show you "how to," provide the handbook or the tools, info, data you need to achieve or learn (think Lowe's®, Rosetta Stone®, or the CDC in the US).

Helper: It will assist you in doing what you need to do, take care of a business need (think Spectrum®), family (think ShopRite®), money (think Citibank®), or home (think Home Depot®).

Reliever: It will relieve your pain or suffering, whether it's an analgesic (think Tylenol®) or a brand stepping up to help during a hurricane (think Tide®).

Brand Storytelling Archetypes

The struggle between good and evil, heroes and bad guys, forces and influences of the universe and nature comprise stories and myths across cultures and continents, providing structures and frameworks for storytellers—filmmakers, novelists, poets, brand storytellers, and advertising creators.

In *The Hero with a Thousand Faces* (1949), Joseph Campbell outlines the Hero's Journey, a universal motif of adventure and transformation that runs through virtually all the world's mythic traditions. From George Lucas's *Star Wars* to J.K. Rowling's *Harry Potter*, Campbell's explorations of comparative mythology have influenced many great storytellers as well as great brand storytellers, advertising art directors, copywriters, and creative directors.

In *The Seven Basic Plots: Why We Tell Stories*, literary theorist Christopher Booker examines the recurring plots of films, opera libretti, contemporary novels, and short stories. He offers five basic archetypal plot structures that have guided storytelling for hundreds of years, plus explanations of comedy and tragedy, which we won't examine because they're too broad, and tragedy doesn't really fit into the advertising or branding genre.

When you evaluate a brand's story, see if any of these archetypes apply:

Overcoming the monster: A hero, the protagonist, faces and conquers an evil force—a "monster" of any kind. Campbell calls this archetypal story, "The Hero's Journey." Here, the hero is called to action by an inciting event. During the arc of the story, the main character rises to face the challenge, taking on the role of a hero. Some people think of this as an underdog story. (Rags to riches also is an underdog story, which is coming up next.) Think *Beowulf, Jaws, Seven Samurai*, and *Star Wars*.

Rags to riches: A main character, an underdog, gains something of worth, for example, wealth, power, privilege, love (e.g., *Aladdin*), acceptance, or something of great value. The character is in jeopardy of losing it, but triumphs in the end. Think *Annie, Charlie and the Chocolate Factory, In the Heights, Jane Eyre*, and *Slumdog Millionaire.*

The quest: The main character is called to adventure, forcing them to leave their ordinary world to fulfill an objective or secure an object, a prize, or even something such as immortality, as in *Gilgamesh*. Often, the hero initially refuses the call but ultimately takes on the quest, encountering many obstacles along the way. Think *Finding Nemo, Lord of the Rings, The Odyssey, Okja, Raiders of the Lost Ark*, and *Ratatouille.*

Voyage and return: The hero leaves their regular world or environment, traveling into the unknown and facing the prodigious challenges of that new world before returning safely home. Think *Alice in Wonderland, Get Out, Moana, Orpheus and Eurydice, Schmigadoon!*, and *The Wizard of Oz.*

Rebirth: The main character redeems themself through trials and tribulations, changing or transforming their essential self, such as Ebenezer Scrooge's transformation in Charles Dickens's *A Christmas Carol*. An event is usually the catalyst for change. Think *Beauty and the Beast, Groundhog Day, Pride and Prejudice*, and *The Power of the Dog.*

Thinking Like a Strategically Creative Art Director

Synergy is an abused buzzword that truly applies to how copy and images optimally work together. Here's a simple way to think about the communication relationship between copy and image (or art): 1 + 1 = 3. Together, the copy and image communicate more than either does alone.

Image/Copy Relationship Constructions

To think like an art director, consider how to best communicate the ad idea to the right audience through the cooperative relationship of copy and image; the style of visualization; the strategic emphasis of the headline or the image; the brand voice as expressed through the imagery, style, and typography; and the way everything is organized to capture people's attention.

> **Art Direction forms the visual voice of a brand, as words form the written or audio voice of the brand. What makes it so crucial is that, with the exception of radio in every other medium, the art direction is always the first and last thing an audience sees in a piece of advertising communication. How it visually announces itself determines whether it will ever be read, and how it impacts our senses will determine whether it will ever be remembered.**
> **—Greg Braun, retired Dep., Global Chief Creative Officer of Commonwealth/McCann**

There are many copy/image constructions. To evaluate whether the relationship is synergistic, become familiar with three of them: copy-driven, image-driven, and emblematic constructions.

Copy-driven Construction

In a *copy-driven* construction, the art director emphasizes the copy (the words or headline) in the form of typography or hand lettering and de-emphasizes images (Figure 6.1). For the headline to be the star, it must be attention-grabbing simply because people tend to prefer pictures over words. The typographic treatment should be appropriate for the audience and the context (where and when it will be seen and how far the ad will be from the viewers [think outdoor board vs. magazine ad]). All art direction choices should strategically serve the idea. There are copy-only ads as well.

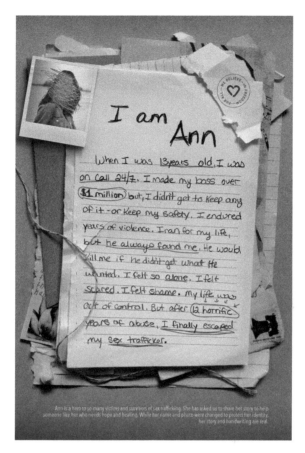

Figure 6.1 Direct Mail (front): "I am Ann"
Designer: Olga Demeshchik
Copywriter: Olivia Santandreu
Client: Free for Life International

According to Free for Life International, "Ann was trafficked for over ten years. She has been served by Free for Life for four-and-a-half years and has been healing and thriving throughout that time. We commend Ann for her bravery in sharing her story to help others like her." Free for Life International is a nonprofit with the mission of the identification, assistance, and restoration of individuals affected by human trafficking and exploitation, working toward a vision of freedom for all. www.freeforlifeintl.org.

Image-driven Construction

In an *image-driven* construction, the art director emphasizes the image and de-emphasizes the headline or copy. The image drives the communication. In this construction, the headline contextualizes and supports (Figure 6.2).

Figure 6.2 Ad Campaign: Ibeu
Agency: Agencia 3
Creative Directors: Alvaro Rodrigues and Luiz Salvestroni
Art Director: Alexandre Collares
Copywriters: Gabriel Gil, Leo Pitanga
Client: Ibeu
"Lots of people move to Brazil after falling in love with the country. But since Portuguese isn't the easiest language to learn, we decided to give them a little hand so they could feel at home in their new country."—Alexandre Collares

There are no-copy ads as well, which work well for audiences where language might be a barrier to message communication. When it is an image-only ad, the image must communicate a clear message flying solo.

Emblematic Construction

In an *emblematic* construction, the image and copy are inseparable. It's a fusion of words and images (see Figure 6.4).

Lodestar Ideas

An *advertising campaign* is a series of coordinated ads based on an over-arching strategy and closely related ideas that are connected by look, feel, voice, tone, style, imagery, and tagline. Each individual ad in the campaign can stand on its own. An *integrated media advertising or branding campaign* works across media channels (Figure 6.3), which might include print, broadcast, interactive, mobile, social, video-sharing, AR/VR, experiential, environmental, other screen-based media, out-of-home media, product design, and unconventional media.

Figure 6.3 Advertising, Branding: BABOON®
Studio: Sagmeister & Walsh
Creative Director: Jessica Walsh
Lead Designer: Daniel Brokstad
Copywriters: Jessica Walsh, Rachel Denti
Designers: Ryan Haskins, Matteo Giuseppe Pani, Chen Yu
Photography/Creative Director, Baboon: Michael Kushner
Photographer, Lifestyle Shots: Blaise Cepis
Photographer, Product Shots: Henry Hargreaves
Client: BABOON
"BABOON is a bags operation for the new generation of travelers. Made for the slash generation, BABOON wanted an identity that was irreverent, flexible, and full of weird surprises. We created the name for the company, the brand identity, illustrations, a custom typeface, social media content, copywriting and more. We also helped suggest product design choices, such as color and illustrations for a set of unique BABOON-branded patterns for the interiors of the luggage. What is the one thing you can guarantee someone will do with a bag? They will open it! We saw the opening of a duffle bag as an opportunity missed by many brands to do something delightful and unusual. Doing something really lovely in the interior helped differentiate BABOON duffle bags from any other bag on the market, especially in contrast with their monochromatic style."—Sagmeister & Walsh

An Ad Idea Must L.A.S.T.

An ad idea must L.A.S.T.:

Lodestar: A "Lodestar" idea is your North Star—your mission and guiding
    light that makes each execution conceptually sound. Would your idea
    make people think or feel something? Change their point of view?
    Always remember to ask: *What's the overarching (Lodestar) idea?*
Attract: It must grab attention; people must notice it.
Shareworthy: People should find it remarkable, relatable, or relevant enough
    to themselves or their community to share it.
Tantalize: It should entice, engage, prompt, or move people to feel, think, or
    do something. Which emotion do you want them to feel? Call people
    to action.

Triplets Versus Cousins

Getting under consumers' radar is a brilliant rule. In *Under the Radar: Talking
to Today's Cynical Consumer*, Jonathan Bond and Richard Kirshenbaum discuss just that. No one wants to be sold to—neither by a pushy salesperson
nor by an ad in any form on any channel. Most people can smell a pedestrian
ad a mile away, whether on Instagram, Twitter, in print, on a billboard, or
on television.

If the art direction is pedestrian in concept, style, layout, typography, and
imagery, then people immediately know it's an ad and are far less likely to
engage. If a single ad looks fresh in concept, style, layout, typography, and
imagery, then it is much more likely people will notice it.

According to Rob Reilly, Chief Global Creative Officer of WPP, "For the
best ideas, you need to have some level of risk or some level of fear that this
won't work."[3] He goes on to describe what he refers to as the Press Release
Process, which Reilly developed when at CPB and employs wherever he
works:

> When the idea lands in culture, what's the story the press will write about it?
> … What's the thing people love and share? What's the thing that's so powerful
> that it becomes part of culture? If you can't write the Press Release, it's prob-
> ably not going to be an idea that works.

If you study ad or poster campaigns, you will notice there often seems to be an underlying compositional structure or template that is employed for individual ad units in a campaign. ("Template" is used here to mean a master layout designed by the art director or designer, not a premade template found in a software program or on a web platform.) When art directors design a master compositional structure or template for a specific campaign, they make determinations concerning type alignments, compositional structures, and positions of elements within the composition, which will be the same or very similar from ad unit to ad unit. I refer to this campaign structure as *triplets* because each composition is identical or almost identical to the others. Many campaigns are designed this way. For each ad unit in a triplet structure, the main image may change, the headline may change, but the compositional structure stays the same or very close to the same. Other elements an art director might maintain are the color palette, typeface(s), method of visualization, style, or images from the same photographer or illustrator.

Carried through any integrated campaign, there is an overarching strategy with related specific ideas conceived for different media channels. Each idea is communicated through the visual and verbal relationship in each individual ad unit for each media channel and each contributes to the brand story. The core Lodestar idea must be flexible enough to sustain a campaign, where every point of contact becomes a compelling experience. To achieve this requires: 1) a compelling story (or piece of the story)—each and every time, and 2) some benefit for the audience, whether it's entertainment, information, or utility—something they want from a brand or entity.

Cousins Versus Triplets

Some art directors prefer to create what I refer to as a *cousins structure*—a campaign where there is a familial appearance; however, each ad unit is not identical to the other. Compared to triplets, there is a greater degree of variation in the composition, color palette, and visualization among the ad units, yet the campaign still holds together and manages to maintain a distinctive appearance. With cousins, *unity with variety* is the goal (see Figure 6.4) to keep people's interest every time they see an ad unit from the campaign.

Figure 6.4 Poster Campaign: "Footy Fans"
Agency: Design Intoto, Sydney
Art Direction/Illustration: Alexandre Collares
Client: KFC
"Aussie footy fans prefer KFC. Since we prefer not to keep that to ourselves, the only reasonable thing to do was spread the word. This campaign was created after a survey found that KFC was one of the favorite fast foods of Australian rules football fans."—Alexandre Collares

Many clients and creatives believe that repetition is crucial, so they tend to prefer triplets across media. Triplets ensure viewer recognition of the brand messages within a campaign. "That looks familiar," some people might think. The campaign doesn't need to reintroduce itself each time. The logic is that the more impressions (the times each ad unit is viewed), the more likely that the message will register and be remembered. Other experts think once viewers have seen one ad unit in a series, they will be bored if the next ad in the campaign looks the same, and they will ignore it.

What Makes a Good Integrated Campaign?

- The campaign is based on a flexible Lodestar idea.
- Each individual ad unit, across media channels, grabs and holds people's attention and compels them to act.

- Each individual ad is conceived and executed for the specific media channel to best connect with people and offer some value to consumers, something worth their time.
- The art direction lends distinction and differentiates the brand from its competitors.
- It ignites a conversation between the brand and people.
- People will talk about it and share.
- The campaign offers entertainment, information, utility, or it does some social good (brand activism).

Worldbuilding

Think of the world of Haruki Murakami's *IQ84*, Wes Anderson's *The Grand Budapest Hotel*, Ava DuVernay's *A Wrinkle in Time*, or Ridley Scott's *Blade Runner*. Generally, in fiction, film, animation, or advertising, worldbuilding is the process of constructing an imaginary world, where the world being created is entirely new and believable in its context—it may even be an entire fictional universe.

Art directors create parameters for visual style, characters, and actions in commercials and online videos, TikTok concepts, any media channel and scenario—a system of rules and behavior guidelines that govern the entire campaign.

At times, brand worldbuilding dovetails with existing fictional worlds built for television programming or another medium, for example, promotions created for entertainment programming.

At other times, agencies and studios build immersive worlds that are unique, such as "The World of Coca-Cola" in Atlanta or LEGO® attractions in theme parks. AMV BBDO/London developed "#wombstories" for client Essity's Bodyform®/Libresse® brands, which won practically every industry award. After AMV BBDO was named Agency of the Festival at the Cannes Lions, Alex Grieve, Chief Creative Officer, commented:

> Being named Agency of the Festival is an incredible honor and doing so with some of our most brilliant work to date, across various clients, makes it even sweeter. Particularly with #wombstories, we've been fortunate to have a fearless client in Essity, who are attuned to the power of creativity and aren't afraid to challenge the status quo. It's been thrilling pushing the creative boundaries with them year-over-year.[4]

Constructing a world around a brand allows for richer stories, including immersive branding, AR/VR, experiential, digital stories, and more, encouraging people to spend more time with brands and fan participation with the built worlds.

Style of a Campaign

Style is a visual look and feel based on the specific graphic or pictorial characteristics that contribute to the overall appearance. Typefaces, color palette, textures, patterns, compositional modes, kinds of images (illustration, photographs, etc.), the nature of the imagery, and graphic elements all contribute to the look and feel of an advertisement or ad campaign across media channels.

Most art directors prefer consistency in imagery and typefaces across a campaign, such as when the creatives employ a similar illustration style for all of the videos or posters in a series. For example, if they utilize black and white imagery in one unit of the campaign, then they use it throughout (Figure 6.5). Furthermore, if the imagery has dramatic light-dark relationships, they are maintained. If color illustrations are used in one ad unit, then they are used throughout (Figure 6.6). The degree of variety will affect how well the campaign holds together in the audience's mind over each ad unit and how each contributes to recognition.

An art director determines what is appropriate for the brand, the core campaign strategy, and the Lodestar idea. Very importantly, the style of visualization should differentiate the campaign from the competition and add freshness, as long as it is appropriate for the brand personality and values.

As Ana Paola Noriega Cid, Chief Creative Officer at FCB Mexico, advises, "An important thing about technology is knowing when not to use it." When I asked her to elaborate, Cid explained,

> This applies to many situations. For example, in art direction, sometimes it is better to do things by hand. It also applies to data analysis—machines need a human characteristic: intuition. And, of course, it applies to life: it is important to have technology to connect, but it is important to disconnect to connect much more deeply.

Figure 6.5 Poster Series: Sea, Land, and Air (aka "Plastic Fish," "Eden," and "Plastic Bird")

Designer/Illustrator: Scott Laserow

"The first in the series was 'Plastic Fish,' which was created for an environmental poster exhibition on plastics and plastic waste. Part of the rules was your image must be black and white. I had never worked in black and white; it turned out to significantly influence my work as I moved forward from this project. The image was inspired by a quote that I ended up using on the poster: '2/3 of the world's fish suffer from plastic ingestion.' Initially, I had no intention of creating a series, but as time passed, opportunities presented themselves to continue the theme to cover Sea, Land, and Air. The series took close to three years to complete, and all the images were executed differently. 'Plastic Fish' was a combination of photos I took and stock imagery. 'Plastic Bird' is a clay sculpture with a wire armature for the wings; each plastic feather was either individually pinned to the plasticine or taped to the wing armature. I then photographed the sculpture and photoshopped details of the beak and the straw legs. 'Eden' was the final poster in the series and was mainly created in photoshop."—Scott Laserow

Aesthetics

"By *style* is meant the constant form—and sometimes the constant elements, qualities, and expression—in the art of an individual or a group," according to art historian Meyer Schapiro.[5]

Style provides a distinctive quality. It can differentiate a brand or entity. Style is a vehicle for expression.

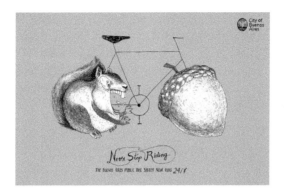

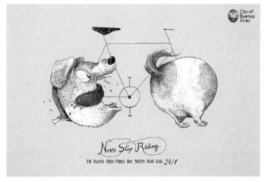

Figure 6.6 Campaign: "Never Stop Riding" City of Buenos Aires
Agency: The Community, Miami
Chief Creative Officers: Joaquín Mollá/José Mollá
Creative Directors: Fernando Reis/Marcelo Padoca
Art Director: Guilherme Nobrega
Illustrator: Arthur D'Araujo
Client: City of Buenos Aires

It's important to differentiate between "style" and one's "taste." "Taste is not only personal. It's also social. Taste both extends from people's lived experiences and gives form to a community's sense of belonging. So, it's important to make aesthetic decisions based on a connection with design audiences," explains Aggie Toppins, Associate Professor at Washington University in St. Louis.

Many designers have philosophies about aesthetics or style—they hold to established schools of thought or work from their own beliefs about the role of design and its form.

> **Professional designers have historically been trained to work with form in a disinterested way, in which the elements and principles of design are seen as tools for accomplishing communicative goals. This tendency has been coupled with a common assumption that designers should impart "good taste" through a modernist sensibility, described as rational, objective, even culturally transcendent. Aesthetics take on a moral dimension in this rhetoric: good design = apolitical, acultural design. I think this is beginning to change. As the field reckons with questions of equity and inclusion, what constitutes "good taste" is beginning to be understood as situated and contingent on the contexts and audiences involved with the work.**
> **—Aggie Toppins, Associate Professor,**
> **Washington University in St. Louis**

You can't help but bring your own taste to your critique of advertising, branding, or graphic design solutions. I had a client who hated green; if you showed her the same layout in blue, she'd approve, but if it was in green she nixed it. Her dislike for green had nothing to do with how I solved the ad problem or with the audience. It was just her preference. This is not a best-practice approach, for sure.

Of course, all creative professionals realize that the brand voice must be paramount. As Ross Chowles says in the interview in Chapter 3, "Neither the designer's nor the client's personal taste level is relevant. The strategy/brand positioning/personality should define the taste level."

Brand Story and Art Direction Efficacy Tool

Ask yourself: Am I ...

- Responding to a color palette based on my personal preferences or based on how it works for the idea, brand, audience, and media channel?
- Preferring a style of photography, video, motion, or illustration because it's familiar? We tend to get used to things and therefore we find them more acceptable over time.
- Open to styles of visualization or layouts I haven't seen before?
- Assessing whether the audience would find it appealing?
- Assessing if it aligns with the brand essence and story?
- Thinking about diversity and inclusion?
- Thinking about representations of power?

Interview with LISA SMITH, Executive Creative Director at Jones Knowles Ritchie

Lisa is the Executive Creative Director at Jones Knowles Ritchie and has over 20 years of creative industry experience. She most recently led the brand transformation of Burger King to help improve its quality and taste perception by using design to make the BK brand and the food even more craveable across the full brand experience. She is the former ECD of Chobani®, where she was responsible for the rebrand across design, packaging, digital, advertising, experiential, partnerships, and innovation. There, Lisa put creativity at the heart of the business, transforming the brand, growing its product offering, and

Figure 6.7 Lisa Smith
Photographer: Mari Juliano

increasing its customer loyalty, directly translating to top-line growth. Prior to Chobani, Lisa was Head of Design at Wolff Olins NY, focused on creating striking, groundbreaking, and commercially successful work, including The Met®, Zocdoc®, Grubhub® and *USA Today*. Lisa has been the recipient of a Gold Cannes Lion, D&AD, The One Show, and Art Directors Club awards. She received Best in Show for Burger King at the *Dieline* and FAB Awards, a Brand Impact Award in Culture for The Met, and a *Fast Company* Innovation by Design Awards for the rebrand of *USA Today*, and many other accolades for her outstanding work. Most recently she judged Cannes Lion Design and Clio Awards, she's been the foreman judge at D&AD's Professional Awards for Graphic Design, and she has also spoken at DesignThinkers and the HOW Creative Summit. Lisa and her work have been featured in *FastCo Design*, *Ad Age*, *Adweek*, *Wired*, *Creative Review*, *Design Week*, *Computer Arts*, *It's Nice That*, the *New York Times*, and more.

How can clients and creatives collaborate to achieve a successful outcome together?

The best creative outcomes lie in the best collaboration between the client and the creatives—whether I've been working agency-side on projects, such as Burger King, The Met, Zocdoc, Grubhub, or *USA Today*, or in-house with a founder and CMO on Chobani.

There must be:

Trust and respect for each other—the client knows their business better than anyone, and the creatives have their expertise that they bring to the table.

An openness—often what starts with a client brief unfolds in the discovery and strategy phase of the project into a true insight and challenge that design can solve.

Shared values—whether that be bravery to do the right thing, a tenacity to strive for the extraordinary, or a desire to be unique by pushing for the brand's differentiation to set them apart from everyone else and truly be themselves.

And, finally, an ambition—to get to the best solution for the brand, even if that means having difficult conversations along the way.

Figure 6.8 Burger King Logo
Design: Jones Knowles Ritchie
TM & © Burger King Corporation

Figure 6.9 Burger King Packaging
Design: Jones Knowles Ritchie
TM & © Burger King Corporation

Figure 6.10 Chobani Logo
Design: Chobani Creative
© Chobani, LLC.

Figure 6.11 Chobani Greek Yogurt Packaging
Design: Chobani Creative
© Chobani, LLC.

Figure 6.12 Chobani Postcards
Design: Chobani Creative
© Chobani, LLC.

Figure 6.13 Grubhub Restaurant Window Vinyl
Design: Wolff Olins

Figure 6.14 Grubhub Brand Identity Illustration
Design: Wolff Olins

Figure 6.15 The Met Logo
Design: Wolff Olins

Figure 6.16 The Met Maps
Design: Wolff Olins

Figure 6.17 Zocdoc Logo
Design: Wolff Olins

Figure 6.18 *USA Today* Logo
Design: Wolff Olins

Figure 6.19 *USA Today* Newspaper
Design: Wolff Olins

What are five collaboration no-no's? Positive approaches?

My five no-no's are:

1. *Pretending you want to collaborate*: I've worked in the industry long
    enough to have seen when creatives say they want to collaborate
    but, really, they think they know best and can be very self-cen-
    tered with their solution. I probably was one of these creatives for
    many years until I worked in-house. The difference in perspective
    gave me empathy to the internal politics of taking an organization
    through a transformation, however big or small, which is no small

task! Having this knowledge now makes me want to strike the balance or design the project that allows for all that internal engagement whilst striving for absolute excellence.

2. *Having too many meetings*: It's great to work with agility and share iteratively as you go, as both sides (agency and brand) can co-create, but this can also mean that there is no time for the unexpected or to push to the uncomfortable zone, which is often when you're onto something truly special. This must be about a balance—give room for the creatives to create and internal engagement to be able to share. There's no right answer here, but I do know when you've had to share every few days and you're working in that constant sprint mode, it leads to the outcome being mediocre and the burnout of the creative teams.

3. *Working in a silo from the rest of the organization*: A brand needs to work out how it can take key stakeholders from the business along for the journey—listening and learning along the way. This still means you need a clear decision-maker on the client side, but navigating this engagement is key to getting the best results with no tissue rejection at the end.

4. *Dismissing the creative if you don't like what you see at first*: Sometimes you hit it out the park and other times it's an iterative process and the work evolves and gets better and better each round. It's a journey, a crooked path of design in fact. On this journey if you can give clear feedback and use design criteria that you co-create from the beginning to remove any subjectivity, judge the work, and continue to develop and refine along the way, then you will get to the best solution. Every project is different, and there can be no guarantee *when* in the process you'll have the answer, but you will get there if the project is designed correctly to do so.

5. *Being kind but not nice*: Healthy challenge along the way is what will create the best work. Whilst it is teamwork, not everyone has to agree. We just have to listen and have empathy for each other's opinions, rationalize, and make a call on what's right for the brand in order to move forward.

I had incredibly positive experiences recently collaborating with the Head of Design at Restaurant Brands International on Burger King. Whilst the original brief wasn't where we took the project, both his and our vision at JKR for the brand couldn't have been more aligned.

We co-created the criteria at the outset, and he gave us the time and the room to create provocations. We did workshops with his key stakeholder group until we landed on mood boards and a direction that felt like the sweet spot for the brand—the right amount of uncomfortableness, but the feeling that you're onto something. We used testing to listen and learn to validate and mitigate, but not to make the decision. He made sure on the BK side they budgeted the right production dollars to develop key assets of the brand—like bespoke type, illustration, motion—to stay as true to the design vision of the brand. And we had the right key moments to share internal engagement with the organization and franchises.

How can clients, business experts, and/or the creatives engage in a useful dialogue? Discuss/critique creative solutions?

It all starts with creating a robust strategy. Building insights around the brand, category, consumer, and culture. This must have the right balance of the truths today, but also looking forward. It culminates in:

- *Purpose*: The organization's reason for existence (which in some cases might already exist and in others needs to evolve).
- *Vision*: What the future looks like if the business is successful.
- *Mission*: How we make the vision a reality.

From this I love a brand idea, design idea, creative platform—whatever the organization might call it—that spearheads the brand personality and creative work across the full brand experience.

Once you have this placemat, it's also useful to create design criteria that can be used as a guide in every single creative meeting to remove any subjectivity and keep everyone focused and on track. The criteria can include:

1. Is it on brand? Does it deliver on the brand idea?
2. Does it stand out? From the competitors but differentiated to the consumers?
3. Is it timeless? Something that feels like it can stand the test of time and doesn't just feel of the moment? You don't want to be revisiting this process every year.
4. Is it practical? Does it work across the brand (consumer) experience today and in the future? Often there is a reason behind why you are

doing this work in the first place, which links to growth and showing up in new ways or new touchpoints, so this can be very important.

5. Does it get people excited? The organization and the consumer?

How can everyone have an integral role?

Assign roles and responsibilities to all collaborators. This is super important. Not everyone has to be in every meeting, and not everyone is the final decision-maker either. Too many opinions can result in the work being diluted to meet everyone's needs and not having the right desired outcome in the end. Does it really matter that one person out of the whole stakeholder team doesn't like the typeface? But strategically it's on point.

How can business people and clients avoid the most cautious (or pedestrian) choices? What's the value of a fresh idea?

If you can land on a brand idea that is distinctive and unique to that brand, then you are already on track. The creative directions become an articulation of this, and they meet the criteria even better. If you need validation, testing can play a role to build a case to the board, investors, or the like. Some of the most senior people in organizations are looking for validation. They understand they are not the experts but want to know how this can help their business grow. So, no CEO partners picking brand colors or the neighbors next door adding opinions ... this is the worst moment a creative can experience if it happens. Just being honest!

What are five points you wish business professionals (business owners, CEOs, clients, marketing teams) understood about the creative side of advertising, branding, and design? Please explain.

1. Fast, cheap, and good doesn't exist. For example, fast and good will cost you, as we'll need double the team to fast-track and deliver at the same level of quality.
2. Empower those who have the most experience working with the creative agency to lead the internal engagement. If you don't have this, talk to the agency about help with this.
3. Set expectations for updates, reporting, and input levels.
4. Budget and put aside a production (execution) budget to develop the brand beyond the creative fee, such as creating distinctive assets like bespoke typography, illustration, and photography style. This often gets overlooked. Brands put production dollars aside for

advertising that's very seasonal and one-off, but often not for brand assets that will stand the test of time.

5. Trust the creative agency's expertise. And expect a bit of give and take.

Any advice on how not to kill a creative idea?

Ask the question: "Does this deliver on the brand strategy?" Use the design criteria to make sure it delivers on the goals. And if you need further validation for senior leadership buy-in, testing can help. Note that testing will never lead you to the most disruptive solution, as consumers will always choose something that feels familiar, but it will mitigate doing anything irresponsible or potentially damaging for the brand. In the end, it's up to the brand to be brave if they really want to grow an audience, stand out, and ultimately grow.

Why are insights into the audience important?

The consumer is at the heart of any brand. I always think that if you can find the ultimate fanbase and bottle up what they love about the brand, then design plays a role in amplifying that. But it's also good to understand what's important to the consumers who don't love or use the brand today in order to know what we aren't doing and how we can get them to reappraise this brand and potentially purchase or use it in the future.

What should business people understand about creating for different media channels?

First, understand your brand experience and the consumer's points of entry to your brand. Second, make sure the media channels that you curate are going to drive consumers directly to a point of entry. I'm not an expert in media channels, but from my time at Chobani I often ask the question: Is the goal to create brand awareness and love—to do something that cuts through culture and garners attention, e.g., an activation or a conversion play—or is the goal something much more commercial—to do something that leads to a direct transaction, e.g., point of sale or banner ads? Sometimes it can be both. And I'm sure I'm oversimplifying.

Historically, brands would choose many creative agencies that specialize in one of these, and the different media channels could look very different to each other depending on whether it was a centralized marketing team on the brand side or much bigger than that. More and more, brand-distinctive assets that are iconic and recognizable need to be the red thread that ties this all together, e.g., the logo, the colors, the typography, the images, the tone of voice, the sound, the movement, etc.

What do you wish your clients understood about diversity, equity, and inclusion (DEI)?

Clients, like branding and advertising agencies, are on a journey of learning and transforming for meaningful and sustained progress in diversity, equity, and inclusion. The creative industries, I'm sure like other industries, need to take action to create an overdue transformation in representation: hiring, training, and growing talent; casting teams; forming partnerships; and making sure there is the correct representation in the work. While the work in DEI space is ongoing, I am proud of the steps we have been taking towards this at JKR.

The difference working at a brand like Chobani—who built their business foundations on DEI and are constantly talking, educating, and celebrating this and making sure it's a priority—is profound. The rest of the world and industry are trying to catch up to examples like this. I'm thankful that clients and agencies together are now talking about DEI, starting to implement action plans, and making sure we hold each other accountable along every step of the way.

Do you show your client more than they ask for? If so, why?

The design process is often very generative, exploring many options along the way, e.g., logos etc., but then we start to filter and get reductive in order to focus in and develop. Some clients might want to be part of this, and others follow very tightly to the process and wait for the culmination of two or three directions with some key touchpoints from the brand experience. Often, we don't do a lot of touchpoints until we're developing just one direction and stress testing the design system across the full brand experience and world. We've often found it counterintuitive to overwhelm clients with things they are not looking for. Less is more in some cases, and it's hard for us to cut down sometimes, too! But then once you are more focused in on one direction, we might start to provoke: What would it be like to create these unique touchpoints for launch and upsell on things, which could really deliver on the direction we are heading and have the most impact from the outset?

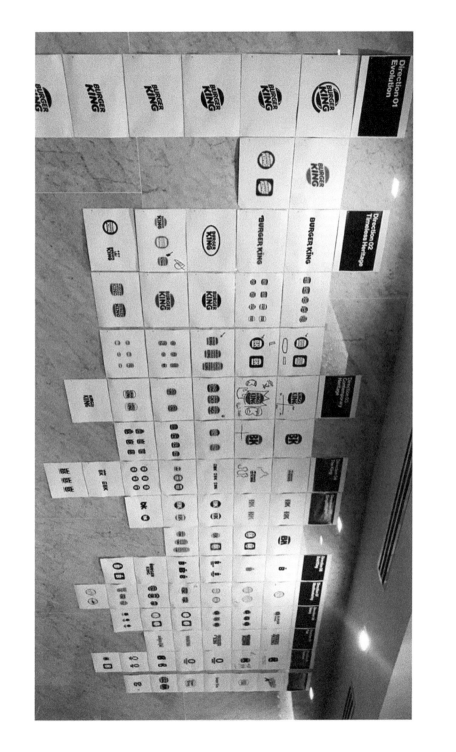

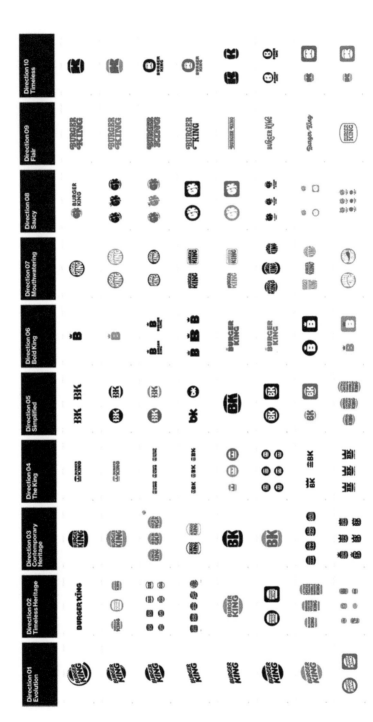

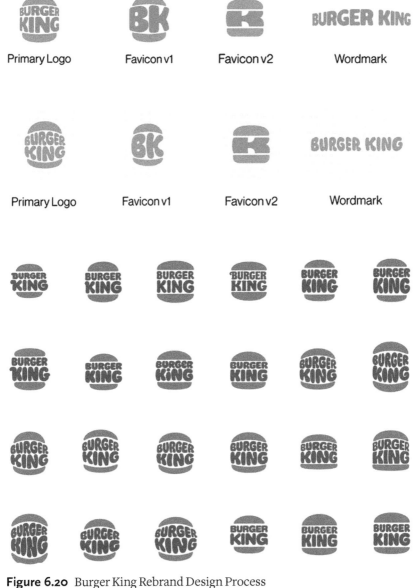

Figure 6.20 Burger King Rebrand Design Process
Design: Jones Knowles Ritchie
TM & © Burger King Corporation

What do you wish clients and business people understood about your job? About branding?

Putting creativity and design at the heart of your business can really transform it and set it up for long-term growth.

It's not a straight path to the solution. It's a journey, and if you don't feel uncomfortable along the way, then you probably aren't onto something that will truly make a difference and impact your business. And don't expect everyone will like it! No one likes change. But change is what keeps us moving forward.

Notes

1   Maham Abedi, "Martin Luther King Jr. took a knee in 1965. Here's a history of the powerful pose," *Global News*. September 26, 2017. https://globalnews.ca/news/3769534/martin-luther-king-jr-take-a-knee-history.

2   "Nike: Dream Crazy," *Effie.org*. https://www.effie.org/case_database/case/US_2020_E-5469-719.

3   "Meet … Rob Reilly, Global Chief Creative Officer, WPP, and Walter Geer, ECD, VMLY&R," *WPP*. June 2021. https://www.youtube.com/watch?v=VFwQsqk_e84.

4   "AMVBBDO London Named Agency of the Festival at 2021 Cannes Lions International Festival of Creativity," *Oneida Daily Dispatch*. June 25, 2021. https://www.oneidadispatch.com/2021/06/25/amvbbdo-london-named-agency-of-the-festival-at-2021-cannes-lions-international-festival-of-creativity.

5   Meyer Schapiro, "Style," in *Anthropology Today*, ed. Alfred L. Kroeber, pp. 287–312. Chicago: University of Chicago Press. 1953.

Having had a front row seat in the design industry, I can say without a shadow of a doubt, having a diverse process leads to superior outcomes. To do that, you must have diverse and capable voices at the table, and they must be heard. Whether it's design, strategy or messaging, the goal is for the final product to resonate with the largest audience possible.

The pitfall of not having representation is that you are creating within a bubble. The biggest danger of that is you're limiting yourself to one corner of a market.

—*Nijel Taylor, Design Director*

Chapter

Diversity, Equity, Inclusion, & Purpose-led Marketing

Diversity, Equity, and Inclusion

Every semester, I require my university creative advertising and graphic design seniors to create a "passion project," a self-directed project that demonstrates an interest in something other than advertising or graphic design. Potential employers want to see evidence of junior talents' interests, and the projects offer fresh takes on subjects while providing insights into their personalities. As Ollie Olanipekun, Founder and Creative Director of Futurimpose, commented, "Show me the stuff you're doing in your spare time. Show me your passion projects. We are really looking for people who can break the mold."[1]

To fulfill her senior passion-project assignment, Danielle Thomas, now a professional designer, created a short film titled "Pretty for a Black Girl." The film deals with microaggressions against Black women today.

Dr. Kevin Nadal, a professor of psychology at John Jay College of Criminal Justice, defines microaggressions as the "everyday, subtle, intentional—and oftentimes unintentional—interactions or behaviors that communicate some sort of bias toward historically marginalized groups."[2] Microaggressions target people based on conscious or unconscious bias; they belittle, demean, and send as well as propagate negative messages.

Kean University aired Ms. Thomas's film during our annual Research Days conference. After showing the film, dozens of women in the audience rushed up to Ms. Thomas to praise her work and say how she had hit a nerve. Ms. Thomas was talking to them about something they were living. Racism, of which microaggressions are a part, isn't driven solely by individual prejudice, but a system of inequity bolstered by unjust laws, policies, politicians, and recirculated discriminations, micro and macro.

By being aware, we can begin the immense challenge of making sure the communication we distribute does no harm—and perhaps even does some social good.

DOI: 10.4324/9781003230786-7

Interrogating Creative Solutions

Dealing with bias requires examining your assumptions and the assumptions of the folks creating the brand or entity's communication. Hope lies in reflection.

By interrogating your own thinking, being mindful of unconscious bias, you start the process of being aware when stereotypic associations are being employed or constructed in conversations, discourse, or creative solutions. The messages we create, shape, and distribute reflect society as well as shape it. We absorb what the messages communicate and put our own responses out there, on social media platforms, on websites, and in conversation. It's a significant challenge to ensure that whatever we send out is responsible.

If you're so inclined, it's useful to take the Harvard Implicit Bias test (implicit.harvard.edu).

Words, Images, and the Stories We Tell Matter

The first time I saw "Killing Us Softly," a lecture and short documentary by media scholar and feminist activist Jean Kilbourne, I was shocked by some of the body-language messages I hadn't noticed prior. I had noticed the sexualized representation of women in advertising and branding—that was hard to miss. But I hadn't been vigilant about spotting subtler portrayals. For example, in one ad for a brand of high-end alcohol, we see the man in the photograph looking straight at the *audience*, but the gaze of the woman, who is standing slightly behind the man with her hands on his shoulders, is directed adoringly at him. Minor grievance? Perhaps, but it sends a message of subordination.

Critical Axis (criticalaxis.org) is a community-driven project from The Disabled List that collects and analyzes representations of disability in media. It points to different tropes and distorted narratives that are regularly used, such as inspiration exploitation (inspiration porn), infantilization, the surprise reveal (viewers are surprised to see that the person who accomplished a feat is disabled), or the gift recipient (a disabled person is on the receiving end of a gift or kind gesture—a virtue signaling device employed by a brand or company that forces the disabled individual to be grateful).

Critical Axis writes,

> Disability is fundamentally diverse, reaching every community across the globe. Yet, the people who are chosen to represent disability are not. For instance, 70% of disabilities are completely invisible, but disability representation in advertising focuses glaringly [on], oftentimes with the camera unjustifiably focused on, distinctive elements of atypical bodies. Most importantly though, we have yet to encounter an ad where the disabled body is neither white (or the dominant group in a culture) nor middle class. We hope this changes soon.[3]

There is a long and well-known history of the sexist portrayals of women in advertising and media, from peddling vacuums and washing machines to housewives, to exploiting women's bodies pandering to the male gaze (and wallet). We tend to think of these insidious clichés as historical accounts of eras gone by, disconnected from the ways that we perform and understand gender today. But harmful gender stereotypes in media have not been eradicated; they've simply evolved and adapted along with mainstream culture. In our scramble to avoid stereotypes about women as housewives and sex objects, we've landed on updated alternatives like the supermom or the carefree working woman who has it all. These modern tropes might seem more normalized, but they are just as problematic because they place unrealistic expectations on women. Stereotypes that capitalize on assumptions or negative portrayals of marginalized people's identities operate as a tool to reinforce their inferior position in society, both in day-to-day interactions and in broader power structures. Portrayals of gender in the media aren't simply a reflection of mainstream views; they are also channels through which we negotiate our own beliefs and behaviors around gender in a society. They have the power to belittle women and invoke violence or, if implemented responsibly, to change views and advance equality.

—Alison Place, Assistant Professor of Graphic Design, University of Arkansas

We have enduring patterns of stereotypes about gender, sexuality, neurodiversity, age, ability, race, ethnicity, and socioeconomic status. They are stubborn patterns. Even now, we see stereotyped portrayals of men in advertising and branding—bumbling men trying to do laundry or care for their children. I suppose they're saying men are not intended to be caregivers or enforcing the role men should not play. Society pays a terrible price for stereotyped representations. Tropes circulate and recirculate to the detriment of all.

Social Responsibility

Creative professionals, marketers, and business professionals who create, produce, approve, buy, and distribute cultural artifacts have a responsibility to all members of society, including those of different races, ethnicities, religions, beliefs, abilities, genders, sexualities, socioeconomic statuses, and ages. Encouraging existing hegemonic systems can be dangerous in communication design, which often *sets out to persuade its audience and can shape thinking.*

Even over the past several years, a time when many people are more aware, we see commercialized work that conveys stereotypic thinking and employs denigrating visual tropes and ideas. Graphic design, branding, and advertising rest on the distinction that words and images in combination become objects of transmission. When designers, copywriters, and art directors turn the combination of words and images into visual communication, their own understanding of equity, inclusion, and social justice serves as a collaborator, making their meaning just or imbuing it with bias, whether unconscious or conscious. Creative professionals who create popular culture and the business people—clients, CMOs, CEOs, marketing professionals, business owners, and all business professionals—who approve, contribute to, and distribute it have a responsibility. Inclusion, equity, and respect need to be a concerted effort.

With that firm belief, I offer a set of investigative queries focused on interrogating 1) ideas, images, and text; 2) power; and 3) appropriation.[4] To critique concepts and creative solutions, these questions are critical because they invite reflection and active participation in creating a just society. At the very least, we must not contribute to the hegemonic systems currently in place through our solutions. View the creative product with this lens.

Interrogating Images and Copy

Interrogate all images and copy for meaning to ensure they do not represent negatively.

- Have you considered how people of different ethnicities or communities may identify with (or react to) what you are creating?
- Have you properly researched stereotypes of the group you are depicting and made a conscious effort to avoid them?

- Is a stereotype or trope being employed relative to ability, race, ethnicity, gender, sexuality, religion, age, or other group?
- Are the imagery and copy respectful? Does any of it denigrate, dehumanize, or diminish any group, even with humor?
- Is it a caricature or a historically offensive portrayal of a group or race? Is it a distortion?
- Is an immutable characteristic used as a punchline?
- Have you tried swapping the image/audience for that of another race, ethnicity, gender, ability, age, sexual orientation, religion, or group? If so, do any stereotypes emerge? Is the image/audience still appropriate?
- If possible, have you sought out an outside perspective?

Interrogating Power

- Who holds the power in your representation? Does the ad purposely exclude or oppress?
- Have you thought about the intersectionality of identities represented?
- Have you thought about how someone of a different group would experience this?
- Does the solution build on a stereotype or trope regarding who holds power and who is subordinate?
- Does the solution contribute to any hegemonic systems of oppression?
- Would any group be marginalized by this representation or message?
- Does it build or destroy?
- Does it punch up or punch down?
- Does the solution read from multiple perspectives?
- Does the solution offer alternative readings?
- Have you tested various scenarios?
- Are you aware of misogyny, misogynoir, and toxic masculinity in the portrayals?

Interrogating Appropriation

- Are you employing another's narrative or culture? Is it yours to appropriate?
- Is cultural value lost due to the representation or idea?
- Are you respecting another culture's traditions and customs, particularly those that are held sacred?
- Is there any suggestion of another culture being less developed than another?
- If employing a narrative or culture other than your own, have you done appropriate research?
- Is it reasonable to assume that members from the culture would represent themselves or their customs in a similar manner?
- Are any aspects of the culture being represented out of context?
- Is credit properly given?

Teams

In increasingly global work environments, embracing diversity should be unequivocal. Diversity and inclusion mean representation. They mean many different voices are recognized, valued, and heard. Equity means different people are included and have a seat at the table. When we embrace the inclusion of people across the spectrum of cultures, orientations, races, ethnicities, abilities, and communities, we bring diverse thinking, which likely leads to a more innovative, creative, or imaginative collective. Studies show diverse perspectives add value and richness.

Working with an inclusive team also opens the team's members to broader experiences. Although recent studies show that opening yourself to multicultural experiences increases creative thinking, you only need to look at people such as Pablo Picasso, Shahzia Sikander, John Birks "Dizzy" Gillespie, or Julie Mehretu to see the effect that has on one's work. Or witness the success of fashion designers who are inspired by different cultures—Jean Paul Gaultier, Michael Kors, Duro Olowu, and Mimi Plange.

> The creative process is special in its ability to produce unique variation from a common starting point. To study this process is to study the importance of not only accommodating difference but the value of diversity, equity, and inclusion in producing meaningful solutions both for and from the widest possible audience.
>
> *—Camille Sherrod, Equity in Action Presidential Fellow, Kean University*

Purpose-led Marketing

> To me, purpose-led marketing is here to stay, and I think that is an important thing. Governments are falling short in their main purpose, which is to help people. What an opportunity for brands to fill the gap and positively impact the world. The challenge is to make these purpose-led ideas disruptive. It's not enough to have a bold initiative. You need to deliver to the world in such an interesting, surprising, and powerful way that it can't be ignored. That's the reason why *Fearless Girl* not only won every award in Cannes, it won and will continue to win in culture every day.
>
> *—Rob Reilly, Global Chief Creative Officer, WPP*

In honor of International Women's Day and to demonstrate that a company with women in leadership performs well, advertising agency McCann New York partnered with State Street Global Advisors to conceptualize and commission Kristen Visbal's *Fearless Girl*, a statue of a girl facing the *Charging Bull* statue on Wall Street. This unconventional ad became a global phenomenon. Tourists and New Yorkers flocked to see the statue. Although it drew some backlash and cries of "corporate feminism," the general public and policy makers, such as former New York City Mayor Bill de Blasio and New York Congresswoman Carolyn Maloney, embraced the "ad." (You can make your own determination, of course.) Eventually, due to its ongoing popularity, NYC moved *Fearless Girl* to a location near the New York Stock Exchange, where large numbers of pedestrians can safely view it.

"If you're not willing to act, there's no sense in getting involved in the game because the people you serve are too smart, too savvy, and will call B.S.,"

Figure 7.1 Photograph: "*Fearless Girl* Facing the New York Stock Exchange"
Photographer: Omar Emera, https://www.omaremera.com

wrote Matthew McCarthy, the CEO of Ben & Jerry's®, in an open letter in
Fortune.[5] I agree. People can detect an inauthentic attempt. For brands to be
authentic activists, they must act responsibly and make social good part of
their mission and actions.

When Ben Cohen and Jerry Greenfield, the founders of Ben & Jerry's, started
their business, they were determined to be a force for good through environ-
mentally sustainable practices and community involvement. And they did it.
Even though they've ceded control of the company, Ben and Jerry continue
to take many stands against social injustice, including a corporate statement
about dismantling white supremacy released in response to George Floyd's
killing.

More and more brands are becoming activists, leading with purpose-led
marketing. Research suggests that people are more likely to patronize the
companies and brands that stand up for the issues the customers align with.[6]

Brands such as Nike (standing for social justice) and L'Oréal Paris® (driving female empowerment) are liked and known for their commitment to purpose, according to Kantar, a leading London-based data, insights, and consulting company: "Reputation, especially for sustainable and ethical purposes, is increasingly a driver for brand growth."[7]

When a brand or entity takes a stand on a social issue or cause, that also means taking a side. There will be people who condemn the side a brand stands with and for, and there will be those who laud it. There's no getting around that. When Nike took a stand for social justice with its campaign for the 30th anniversary of "Just Do It" and featured Colin Kaepernick as the face of the brand, controversy erupted. Some customers burned their Nike wear, posting their actions on social media. However, Nike sales defied the backlash and, of course, Nike was seen as an upstander on this issue. In announcing the relationship, Nike said Kaepernick was "one of the most inspirational athletes of this generation." Social media posts for *Colin in Black & White*, the Netflix series created by Colin Kaepernick and Ava DuVernay that follows Kaepernick's life story, proclaimed: "Some people play the game. Others change it."[8]

Whether a brand takes a stand and puts resources behind it, contributes to community, or works towards sustainability, purpose-led marketing must walk the talk.

Social Responsibility Evaluation Scale

- **Damaging**: Will harm society due to bias or stereotypical representations or concepts.
- **Ignorant**: Uninformed concepts and portrayals of people and issues. Oblivious to social issues.
- **Needs scrutiny**: Requires further examination and research for messaging and potential effects on people and society.
- **Provocative**: Not inflammatory but could cause controversy. Takes sides on an issue.
- **Intelligent and respectful**: Considered representations of groups and communities and civil concepts that do no harm.
- **Does good** for society.

People expect brands and corporations to respond to major political, social, or cultural controversies, especially people from younger, diverse demographics and more progressive psychographics, who see their purchases as more than transactional. This offers brands, companies, and other entities an opportunity to demonstrate their values, take action, and make an impact.

Brands and companies have a responsibility to step up as a force of good for society, which will in turn be a force of growth for business. "People are looking at what's behind the brand: What are its values and beliefs, and what are the specific actions they're taking to make the world a better place," according to Marc Pritchard, Chief Brand Officer at Procter & Gamble.[9] As marketing journalist Michael Applebaum explains, "Some marketers argue the more, the merrier when it comes to brands that champion vital causes like the environment."[10] Cory Bayers, VP of global marketing at Patagonia®, agrees,

> It's great to have more voices be a part of this movement because there needs to be a sense of urgency [about climate change] … There are always going to be a few superficial campaigns here and there, but I have confidence in the community and our customers that they know when someone is just trying to appease them or sell them something.[11]

People learn from what they see in popular culture. Let's make sure they're learning respect and inclusion.

Interview with RICH TU, Vice President of Digital Design for the MTV Entertainment Group at ViacomCBS

Figure 7.2 Rich Tu
Photographer: Xavier Guerra

Rich Tu is the Vice President of Digital Design for the MTV Entertainment Group at ViacomCBS. Also, he hosts the Webby Honoree podcast *First Generation Burden*, which focuses on intersectionality and diversity within the creative industry. Rich is a first generation Filipino-American and award-winning artist residing in Brooklyn, NY. He is a graduate of SVA's Illustration as Visual Essay program and received the ADC Young Guns award, which recognizes the world's best creatives under the age of 30. Creatively, his focus is on emerging audiences and energetic brands that benefit from an eclectic and unique point of view. Rich's clients and collaborators include the *New York Times*, the *New Yorker*, *Business Week*, Alfa Romeo®, Bombay Sapphire®, G-Shock®, Nike, Adidas®, Converse®, American Express®, NPR, The North Face Purple Label, Coca-Cola®, Verizon®, Skype®, Fuse TV, and *Hamilton the Musical*, among others. Also, he has exhibited at galleries and festivals in New York, Los Angeles, Berlin, as well as the SCOPE Miami festival during Miami's Art Basel week.

Why should everyone in the visual communication industries aim to amplify diverse voices?

The creative industry overall is an echo chamber, and we often revisit the same people and pieces for inspiration. The unfortunate repercussion is that we reinforce the same aesthetic, creative, and representational ideals and are wary of change, which leads to a bottleneck of emerging voices at the academic and professional levels. Fortunately, there are quite a number of new platforms and tools that lead to breakthrough, so that creatives from historically underserved communities can leverage new tools and also create their own spaces.

Advertising, branding, and graphic design have pretty much always been Euro-centric and male-dominated (at least at the top). What should people understand about this and why it's not only limiting but bad for business?

From a business perspective, white, cis, heteronormative males are not the only audience with disposable income, and only in recent history do we see the positive financial impact of acknowledging communities of color and LGBTQIA+ communities.

From a creative perspective, it's overall limiting, repetitive, and exclusionary, prohibiting progressive thought (i.e., fresh ideas).

From a personal perspective, it's kind of boring at the end of the day.

How can we avoid stereotyping and (at times) racist or offensive marketing?

There's a thin line between acknowledging someone for who they are (which is great), and tokenizing (which is not). I think of the concept "with, not for," which is often used when building inclusive spaces. Collaboration is key. Understanding the needs of a community does not come from a one-sided approach.

We need to build inclusivity together and have these active and occasionally difficult conversations. There's no single right answer, and all the stakeholders need to be at the table.

What is your view of brand activism?

Audiences want to engage with brands that have a point of view that they can identify with. That said, social justice, politics, and identity-based activism occupy a huge part of the media, corporate, and content landscape.

If a brand can gracefully weave social justice into their strategy without it feeling force-fed or extraneous (and there's a lot of that out there), I'm all for it.

Any advice on how business and creative professionals can best discuss creative solutions?

The way we discuss and pitch creative solutions hasn't necessarily changed, but the types of solutions have because the audience is so diverse and highly aware on a community and local level. I would say keep close tabs on where communities congregate and connect (IRL and virtually). If you can speak knowledgeably about how a solution can affect both a community and an individual, you can do A LOT.

What are five essential questions about power, identity, intersectionality, appropriation, dehumanization, and systemic racism that business people should ask when critiquing and judging strategies or creative solutions?

1. "During this process, was there an opportunity for everyone to contribute?"
2. "For this solution to win, does someone have to lose?"
3. "Is this community telling their story?"
4. "Would I be proud to take a snapshot of this 'table' I've set?"
5. Most importantly, "Who are we missing?"

Interview with OLU ADEWALURE, Art Director at The Bloc

Figure 7.3 Oludamilola Adewalure
Photographer: Sofia Philogene

Oludamilola Adewalure, also known as Olu, is a Nigerian-raised creative based out of New Jersey. Olu spent four years at the Robert Busch School of Design at Kean University getting his degree in Graphic Design: Interactive Advertising. Making the design industry a better place for all has always been one of Olu's main motives in his young career. He also believes that working in a fun environment is beneficial to carrying out assignments, so you'll always see Olu moving and grooving while working. Olu started his career as the first ever intern at IDEO.org's New York office. After graduating, he landed his first job at Wunderman Thompson Health as a Junior Art Director, and now he is an Art Director at The Bloc. When Olu is not spending his time creating breathtaking work, he's either spending time with his family, watching anime, or playing video games. There are many different pieces to the amazing puzzle of Olu, but this is just scratching the surface to his young, bright life.

What are two or three points you wish business professionals (business owners, CEOs, clients, marketing teams) understood about the creative side of advertising, branding, and design? Please explain.

It takes time! During my short time working in the ad agency world, I've noticed that some business professionals view creatives as machines. They want solutions quickly and don't realize that they are sabotaging quality. The creative mind does not work as efficiently when under tight turnarounds. To really come up with an idea that resonates with the audience, it's best when the ingredients get to sit in the slow cooker.

Why run with a strategic and novel (creative) idea rather than a "tried and true" idea that has worked in the past?

To put it simply, "Dare to be great." The world is changing insanely quickly every single day, so there's really no time to keep the same "tried and true" ideas.

Inclusion is one of the main driving forces for change today, and most new ideations are aligned with that. Being confident, being bold, being proud, and being inclusive are all attributes that companies/brands/agencies should aim to reach. It's not about what you do, but how you do it!

As a young creative practitioner, you have a fresh perspective. What would you like to see happen in advertising?

Personally, I would love to see more Black people in higher positions in the industry. I would love for there to be more Black-owned agencies, as well. I wholeheartedly believe that there needs to be a bigger shift in leadership; and it starts from there. Seeing more Black people in higher positions and more Black-owned agencies will increase the number of Black creatives as well. It's getting a bit better, but then again it depends on the agency. At the first agency where I worked, I was one of five Black people in the office of 600 employees. At my current agency, there are about 20 of us out of 100 or so. I love the progress.

How can all of us in this industry work towards ensuring diversity, equity, and inclusion (DEI)? What do business people, clients, and creatives need to do/know about DEI?

I think the way industry can work towards ensuring diversity, equity, and inclusion is by practicing open-mindedness. A lot of people in the industry come from or are raised by generations who may not understand the lifestyles of minorities and the cultural differences. To be fully inclusive is to be able to receive and accept others for who they are and where they come from. There are instances where people try to be open-minded but with the wrong approach. Another issue is awareness. For example, although you may be genuine, it is not appropriate to touch someone else's hair. It is also not appropriate to try to create conversation with someone based on a trope or stereotype. There was an instance where a coworker of mine and I were talking about music. I asked what his favorite genre is, and he replied, "I love R&B, how about you? I bet you love rap music and the Migos." At first, I was severely shocked by his reply, but I had to approach the situation instructively, letting my coworker know that their comment was unacceptable. If the industry could work towards being more open-minded and aware of what's going on in the world, we would be doing great.

What should everyone involved understand about hopping on cultural moments? About co-opting pop culture?

Be careful not to be named culture vultures. There are many brands that live off pop culture just for clicks and engagements. Today's society is more aware of companies like that and are being vocal about it. So, if you want to talk the talk, you must walk the walk.

You're into fashion. What have you learned about style and creativity in fashion that you bring to your work?

I learned that style and creativity are very personal. Everyone's life experiences contribute to how they view the world. So, for myself, I like to include a piece of me in everything that I do (and wear). Doing so gives your work more flavor—it feels more alive!—rather than just following a brief and executing dry deliverables.

What do you consider when you're creating content to grab people's attention?

I usually consider other ads that caught my eye (or pop culture's eye) and dissect them. Asking, Why did I like it? Why was this piece created? Why is this a problem/solution? Why, why, why? Once I ask myself all those questions, I keep those questions and answers in the back of my mind when I am creating. I also ask, Does this interest me or am I just executing what is on the brief? I strive to make ideas that make people go, "Ahhhh, I never thought of it that way." The only way to get that to happen is by asking, *Why?*

Your ideas grow businesses. How do you get your ideas? Do you need time to allow your thoughts to incubate?

I am very weird when it comes to getting new ideas. At first, I try to think of pain points I experience with a piece of technology, or I think of a solution for a service that a company offers. After that I watch random recommended videos on YouTube, binge anime, or watch animal documentaries—anything that gets my mind off what I am trying to do. Usually, if I focus too much on generating a new idea, it prohibits me from actually coming up with something fresh. Then, before I go to bed, I say to myself five times: *What would you like to see happen?* By morning

I have a slight idea, and I start writing notes. But there's no rush to be creative, we all operate differently.

Because we never know where the next idea will come from, how can leadership ensure inclusivity and that everyone is heard?

A good leader doesn't dictate. A good leader works with their team and commits to the same actions as them. When that is happening, it makes it easier for the team to approach their leader and makes the leader understand their team more. Someone who hasn't experienced the same thing that I have will never be able to fully understand me. My mom always tells me to "Lead by example." And that can't be done on the sidelines.

What advice would you give someone struggling with their voice in the industry?

Start small and take it day by day. Throughout my childhood, I was bullied without even saying a word; so, all my life I struggled with my voice being heard. It wasn't until I got a bit older that I realized I am not going to allow anyone to dim my light any longer. But it was a progression—it doesn't happen overnight. I repeat, it will not happen overnight! Pace yourself and constantly remind yourself, "I am here for a reason and that reason must be known."

What advice do you have to those who want to improve their critique etiquette?

I feel as though it is important that people know that creatives love to grow, and one of the best ways to grow is from constructive criticism. Often, those that are in the position to critique creative work just give blanket statements and misleading directions. I believe the greater the feedback, the greater the work, and the greater the work, the greater the team. Instead of expressing how much you may dislike an execution, discuss ways that it can better fulfill the needs of the brief.

Notes

1   Kate Magee, "What Do ECDs Look for in Creative Recruits as the Job Market Rebounds after Covid?" *Campaign.* July 12, 2021. https://www.campaignlive.co.uk/article/ecds-look-creative-recruits-job-market-rebounds-covid/1721751.

2   Andrew Limbong, "Microaggressions Are A Big Deal: How To Talk Them Out And When To Walk Away," NPR.org. June 9, 2020. https://www.npr.org/2020 /06/08/872371063/microaggressions-are-a-big-deal-how-to-talk-them-out-and -when-to-walk-away.

3   "Diversity," *Critical Axis*. https://www.criticalaxis.org/trope/diversity.

4   See also, Robin Landa, *Advertising by Design: Generating and Designing Creative Ideas Across Media*, 4th ed. Hoboken, NJ: John Wiley & Sons. 2021.

5   Ellen McGirt, "Corporate America, We Need to Talk about Activism," *Fortune*. January 15, 2021. https://fortune.com/2021/01/15/corporate-america-activism -ben-jerrys.

6   Abdel Aziz, "Global Study Reveals Consumers Are Four to Six Times More Likely to Purchase, Protect, and Champion Purpose-Driven Companies," *Forbes*. June 17, 2020; Zeno Group, "2020 Zeno Strength of Purpose Study," *zenogroup.com*. June 17, 2020. https://www.zenogroup.com/insights/2020-zeno -strength-purpose.

7   "What Are the Most Valuable Global Brands in 2021?" *Kantar*. June 21, 2021. https://www.kantar.com/inspiration/brands/what-are-the-most-valuable -global-brands-in-2021.

8   Ava DuVernay (@ava), "Some people play the game. Others change it," Twitter post, October 12, 2021; Netflix (@Netflix), "Some play the game. Others change it," Twitter post, October 29, 2021. https://twitter.com/netflix/status /1453889320742490113?lang=en-GB.

9   Michael Applebaum and Ad Age Studio 30, "A Politically Divided America is Forcing Brands to Choose Sides," *AdAge*. May 28, 2021. https://adage.com/article /member-content/politically-divided-america-forcing-brands-choose-sides /2332031.

10   Michael Applebaum, "A Politically Divided America."

11   Michael Applebaum, "A Politically Divided America."

Creative collaboration between ad agency and client is rooted in strategy. One of their principal goals is to discover the key insight that forms the foundation for a creative campaign. What drives consumer interest in your brand? What are users' underlying motives? In doing so, it seems obvious to chase the question of what consumers think about your brand. However, the question really should be what consumers think about themselves when they encounter the brand. This is not easy to identify and requires in depth study of the consumer, how they make decisions, what matters to them, and so on. Only then can creative campaigns truly speak to the target market.

—*Jennifer Chang Coupland, Clinical Professor of Marketing, Smeal College of Business Administration, Penn State*

Chapter 8

Building a Culture for Results

Collective Purpose

"Why are we all here?" asked Dan, the CMO of the multinational pharmaceutical company for which I was consulting. We all looked at one another—marketers, creative directors, art directors, copywriters, strategists, brand managers, and creative technologists. Then Dan looked at me, expecting a response, and then everyone looked at me.

"Purpose and collective effervescence," I said. Purpose would move our thinking and solutions from requisite to strategic. Sharing purpose would add collective effervescence, a concept identified by sociologist Émile Durkheim to describe the sense of drive and synchronization people feel when they come together in a group around a shared purpose, whether they are colleagues in a question-storming session or teammates in a sport.

"Yes! Our collective purpose is to strategically build this brand. Let's move forward with this common purpose as a group. Take it from here, Robin," Dan said and left the room.

The Power of Purpose

A shared-goal mindset yields better results. Though it is challenging to cooperate harmoniously when a team is composed of people with very different expertise and inclinations, or when the decision-makers have different expertise than the experts who conceived and crafted the creative solutions.

Creative professionals and business professionals are essentially trained to think in particular ways, with little crossover. By nature, the creative professions and the business professions may naturally attract different types of personalities or thinkers, which compounds the differences. This works against organic collaboration. Clearly, it's critical to avoid an us-versus-them paradigm.

That's why it's important to set optimal conditions for cooperation, communication, and collaboration, which include a well-defined critique guide, a supportive ecosystem, transparency, a central (or key) directive, and mutual respect for everyone's unique skillset.

DOI: 10.4324/9781003230786-8

Culture of Positivity Yields Productivity

Imagine staying up all night to take hold of a principle.

Fifteenth-century Italian artist Paolo Uccello was consumed by his interest in perspective and would stay up all night in his study trying to grasp the exact vanishing point to create a feeling of depth in his paintings. This is according to Giorgio Vasari, a sixteenth-century Italian artist and probably the first biographer of fine artists, who wrote about Uccello in his book *Lives of the Artist*.

In his biography of French nineteenth-century painter Georges Seurat (most famous for his work *A Sunday Afternoon on the Island of La Grande Jatte* (1884), now housed at The Art Institute of Chicago), Pierre Courthion writes that Seurat often worked long into the night.

> When I was studying advertising, I learned something that has always been in the back of my mind: Every client receives the communication they deserve. To receive good communication, the first thing to do is have an agency where you pay for thinking and not for obeying. Secondly, being generous with the data. Thirdly, having a great relationship and creating space to exchange ideas and talk openly. Next is time. We work in an industry where everything was for yesterday, and to come up with better solutions, it is essential to use the time to think rather than to run. Finally, empathy and respect, understanding that creative and production processes are different from other processes and that nothing is that simple.
>
> —*Mariana Peluffo, Executive Creative Director, Cheil Worldwide*

And then there's the famous story from ad man/graphic designer George Lois, who tells of threatening to jump out of the window to save his ad campaign for Goodman's Matzos. You can watch him tell the story in *The Real Mad Men and Women of Madison Avenue*, a PBS program available online.[1]

Why share these anecdotes? Creative professionals often are driven people—they persist when others might not. And no matter how often you say that you're criticizing their work and not them, it's challenging for creative professionals not to take criticism personally when solutions are produced with artistic passion. With that in mind, as well as the belief that we approach all ideas in the workplace with respect, it's best to build a culture for results.

Nijel Taylor, a design director, advises,

> My relationship with design has evolved over my career. Today, I circumvent the traditional creative process where individual contribution and control are front and center. I have pivoted to letting others into my process of making. This subtle shift to a more confident, team-oriented approach has yielded better, more confident work. As a designer, I have learned that the best ideas stem from the most inclusive teams. When a designer works in an environment where the conditions for success are present, you create an atmosphere of psychological safety for creatives to contribute more openly.

Tell us what we need to solve, not how to solve it. Otherwise, you're just getting a more polished version of what you could do alone. When you let us do the solving, you're getting all the additional smarts and creativity that you paid for. This is true at the beginning of a project as well as when you're giving feedback.
—Leigh Muzslay Browne, Creative Director, GSD&M

Jason Alejandro, a graphic designer, art director, and Assistant Professor of Graphic Design at The College of New Jersey, advises,

> It's my belief that clients should be as forthright as possible with the designers or creatives that they've hired or with whom they are working. It's not uncommon for clients, or anyone really, to have trouble finding the right words to express their tastes or preferences about creative work—whether aesthetic or strategic in nature. But being as straightforward as possible without being downright insulting is the way to go. Clients should not only communicate what it is that they dislike, they should also explain why they dislike it. It can be very helpful to also include the things that they do like about the work. If the client is still struggling to find the words to say, they may want to consider metaphors or analogies to help them. They may even want to show some visuals to aid in the discussion. At the end of the day, the relationship between the client/consultant is like many other relationships where sincere and thoughtful honesty is the best way to move the conversation (and the work!) forward.

Trust is earned. Colleagues who trust each other work better together and are more productive. Creative collaboration requires trust. Thinking without a playbook, which fosters creative (twists on existent ideas and things) and imaginative (original) thinking, requires trust.

I prefer thinking without a playbook, meaning thinking as if there are no rules; however, the process of critique works much better with one.

Creative Solutions Discussion Playbook and Critique Guide

Clinical psychologist Dr. Jill Bellinson spoke with me about critiques:

> Once a campaign is designed, it's going to be judged. One must have a thick enough skin to be rejected at that point and to listen to what didn't work so the next round can be better and therefore better received. When the creative process is supportive, rejection in this round is easier to take.

To avoid conflict and emotional responses, a critique process with clear guidelines for assessing creative solutions works much better.

Critique Guide

Keep it Professional

- *Stick to the brief*: Does it meet the team's shared goal(s) and objectives? Consider the *overall strategic plan*, as well.
- *Speak to the audience truth*: Does it respond to the *insight* into the audience?
- *Scrutinize for the brand's overarching essence, voice, and story*: Does it build the longer-term brand narrative?
- *Employ proper terminology*: Utilizing professional terms moves the discussion forward because everyone is on the same page when discussing the solutions or ideas. Avoid "I don't like it." That doesn't help build a strategically creative outcome. Instead, use terms such as *composition, visual hierarchy, balance, focal point*, and *color palette* as well as typographic terms when discussing the design. When discussing the idea, brand messaging, and copy, use proper terminology such as *insight, strategy, Lodestar idea, brand narrative, brand voice, storyline, call to action*, and so on.
- *Determine that it is a strategically creative solution*: Finally, and importantly, is it fresh? Does it engage or surprise? Will the creative solution differentiate the brand or entity? Will people notice it and engage?

Interaction Tactics

- *"Be positive and diplomatic,"* advises Dr. Bellinson. "Other people may not respond in kind, but they're sure to respond negatively to someone who has treated them with negativity."
- *Be open.* Listen more and talk less.
- *Offer broad criticism* or general insights if you're not the creative professional. Susan Daniels-McGhee and Gary Davis, who research creative teams, advise that specificity helps people visualize.
- If you offer your own ideas, be *diplomatic and low-key.* It's best practice to not impose your ideas over the ideas shown to you—make your ideas seem organic to what you're discussing. As Rei Inamoto, Founding Partner of I&CO, advises, "Because, if you want to prescribe a solution, you should do it yourself."
- Recognize that *everyone has a specialized skillset.* The way you respond to the ideas and solutions of others, process information, and engage in discussion is often determined by your specific training, education, how you understand the world, and how the world reacts to you. All of us are shaped by many forces. When evaluating creative solutions, realize that there are differences in expertise. Hopefully, there will be mutual respect for each other's knowledge.
- Keep the shared goal in mind when giving notes. When I work as a consultant, one of the first points I make is to explain that all my "notes" (as a film director would give) are offered to make the work better, not to belittle or show how smart I am. It's never about me; it's always about the shared goal.
- *Be respectful.* Belittling, micro-aggressive comments, or sarcasm doesn't move discussions forward.
- Be aware of *taste.* Determine how you're arriving at your opinion. As Aggie Toppins, Associate Professor of Design at Washington University in St. Louis, advises, "Taste is not only personal. It's also social. Taste both extends from people's lived experiences and gives form to a community's sense of belonging. So, it's important to make aesthetic decisions based on a connection with design audiences."
- *Resist a premature resolution.* If you have some time, sleep on it. My clients and students usually want immediate feedback; however, when I sleep on what I've seen or heard, I always offer better advice or critiques. Something about allowing my unconscious mind to mull it over works well.

Dr. Bellinson told me that one way to develop empathy is to listen.

> Be curious—try to figure out what makes the other person think or act the way they do. What information do they have that leads them to believe what they believe? What past experiences have they had that leads them to present that point of view? What do they value that might be different from my values or priorities? Find their strengths—everyone has some—and something about the person that you can actually like, or at least respect.

> It can also be useful to recognize the places you'll never agree. A religious person and an atheist are always going to disagree about spiritual issues, but they might come together on Renaissance painting. An athlete and a couch-potato won't find a leisure activity they share, but they might agree about a good place to have dinner. Finding the place of agreement is useful; acknowledging the places of difference is even more important.

> **As a branding agency owner, and after being in the branding business for over 25 years, I've experienced a few common client traits with our most successful projects. Clients are enthusiastic and understand the long-term benefits of a successful branding initiative. Clients respect and truly value the creative team's thinking based on a proven portfolio. Clients who provide articulate and constructive commentary about the work will gain the respect of the creative team— because creative collaboration always leads to more impactful outcomes.**
>
> *—Lou Leonardis, Partner/Creative Director, Trillion*

Results Assessment Tool

- *Lodestar Idea*: Identify the conceptual framework or guiding idea. There must be a Lodestar idea, otherwise it's too vague or does not respond to the brief's goal.
- *Art Direction*: The selection of imagery, color palette, typography, composition, and talent should all point to appropriate messaging.
- *Design*: The imagery and typography tell a cooperative story, differentiate, and are on-brand and in sync with the brand's essence, voice, and larger narrative.
- *Shareworthy*: Would people share it on social-media platforms? Would they create user-generated content about it?

- *Authentic to the Brand Narrative*: It is on point with the broader brand narrative in terms of mission, values, voice, and actions.
- *Audience*: Listen carefully to what the audience wants. How does your brand's story connect to them? As John Maeda, a graphic designer, author, and technologist (maedastudio.com), says, "What I've seen is a leader doesn't start with storytelling, they start with story listening."
- *Ignites Convo*: Would people talk about it on social media? Would it capture media attention? Would pundits write about it? Would talk-show hosts mention it? Would people talk about it at the watercooler? Over the dinner table?

> **If the core purpose and strategic rationale is authentic, collaboration can be a powerful tool. There's the "1 + 1 = 3" effect, whereby two brands with distinct but disparate propositions can align around a common cause, solve a consumer friction point together, or even bring an entirely new concept to market. For larger businesses, collaboration can spark greater agility and innovation. Look at how many Fortune 500 companies have been acquired or filed for bankruptcy in the past 20 years. With start-ups chomping at their heels, standing still is not an option for many incumbents, which means that prototyping or co-creating with more nimble and less risk-averse partners can be a vital way of navigating the immediate future.**
> —*Paul Kemp-Robertson, co-founder of marketing advisory service Contagious and co-author of* **The Contagious Commandments: Ten Steps to Brand Bravery** *(Penguin Business)*

A Supportive Environment

From leadership to the person answering the main phone line, everyone at a company or any entity must be respectful and earn trust. When I asked Dr. Bellinson how cross-disciplinary team members can productively and diplomatically discuss creative solutions, she replied,

> Trust is vital for good working relationships and very hard to build. Like nurturing environments (or is trust what makes for nurturing environments?), employees who trust each other work better together and are more productive. But you can't demand trust—you have to build and earn it. The way to build trust is to be trustworthy; the way to earn respect is to be respectful. So, any team member who enters the collaboration distrusting the other workers

or (as so many do) with contempt for other disciplines will fail to inspire trust or collaboration from those other workers.

Creative Collaboration: In S.Y.N.C.

For *creative collaboration* people need to be in S.Y.N.C.:

Strategic Communication: Generate ideas through civil discourse and exchange.
Yes and…: Build on someone's else's thinking and do not shut down discourse.
Nimble Thinking: Experiment through a discovery-driven process, the flow of relevant ideas, responsive pursuit, reflection, modification, and fine tuning.
Cooperate: Work towards mutual trust, shared goals (with transparency), and respect for each participant's expertise.

With that in mind, as well as the belief that we approach all ideas in the workplace with respect, it's possible to build a culture for strategically creative results.

Interview with NIREY REYNOLDS, Director of Creative Impact, North America at McCann Worldgroup

As Director of Creative Impact, North America at McCann Worldgroup, NiRey Reynolds works along with the Co-Chief Creative Officers, North America, primarily supporting the creative department by organizing and nurturing creative ideas. She also is the liaison for awards and creative industry initiatives. Prior to this role, NiRey was the Education Manager at The One Club for Creativity, the world's foremost nonprofit organization recognizing

Figure 8.1 NiRey Reynolds

creative excellence in advertising and design, producing The Young Ones Student Awards and heading the Education Department. Outside of work, NiRey donates her time to diverse young creatives who want to enter advertising/creative industries. Currently, NiRey is the Senior Producer for D&AD SHIFT with Google, a fully funded, industry-led night school program for emerging creatives. Born and raised in New York City, NiRey earned her bachelor's degree from Loyola University New Orleans before returning to New York to earn a master's degree in Branding and Integrated Communications at The City College of New York.

When a CEO or client asks the creative team to create something just like the advertising another brand has distributed, how do you navigate that situation?

The key is for you to be able to identify what it is that they are really asking you to recreate. Is it the use of a happiness-inducing color palette? A heartwarming message or impactful mission? Strip away the noise of the old campaign to clarify the goal.

Any advice on how not to kill a creative idea? How can business people be open to solutions they hadn't anticipated?

In this fast-paced creative industry business people should be receptive to ideas beyond their scope of thinking. Doing our best not to kill creative ideas is what allows out-of-the-box solutions to be born. Clients and creatives should mutually work on their trust. The client needs to believe that the creative can see beyond the ask and is seeking to elevate the brand. The creative, on the other hand, has to respect that the client knows their brand and is invested to the point that they are protective, in creative terms, wanting to keep it safe. This dynamic reminds the client that the business of the agency—and particularly the group—is to create magic, therefore, something outside of what they originally envisioned.

Please offer advice on how to diplomatically explain that "everyone" is not the audience.

Understanding your target audience is one of the most important parts of a campaign. You will find, however, that some business people think "everyone" is an audience to cater to; this is not the case. It is natural to want to capitalize on your product and market it to as many people and in as many places as possible. However, the more targeted your audience the better the messaging. The account team should utilize the resources in their arsenal to support this messaging. Data is a great tool to help break down in numbers how different audiences think and consume in our world. Another more human method to convey the same message is through focus groups, which allow the client to observe feedback from a diverse group of people to bring to the surface how varied their voices and needs are.

How can companies and brands build trust and authentically become allies? Also, please talk a bit about appropriation.

Companies and brands can build trust and authentically become allies with their audiences when they genuinely understand that *allyship* is a verb. The support and efforts demonstrated at a time of crisis need to be consistent to be impactful and build the necessary relationship with consumers. On another note, businesses should do research and get feedback on their diversity plans and how the audience feels to prevent faux pas like appropriation. What one perceives as an effort might offend another.

On representations of power: How can people become more sensitive to how identities are represented or marginalized?

Representation is a word as powerful as its meaning. I want everyone who is reading this right now to think back to their youth and all the media that had an impact on them. How many actors, characters, or models looked like you or had families that looked like yours? How many times were you included? Know that not everyone had the luxury of these experiences. In the United States, this melting pot of cultures, ideals, and nationalities, not everyone has representation on public platforms. We have the ability in this industry to show not only diversity but people in positions of power, and we need to realize the impact these decisions have. There are children who have never had a teacher who looks like them—can you imagine what effect you can create by showing them the potential of their lives?

What do you wish clients and business people understood about being a creative director (or creative professional)?

There is much to be understood about creatives by clients and business people. Primarily that there is a creative process, and the idea is not going to arrive fully packaged with a bow on top. By that I mean a full campaign is not created in an instant. Ideas need time to germinate and take root, much like a seed. Be open to different perspectives and ideas.

Interview with DONALD R. MARKS, PsyD, Associate Professor, Advanced Studies in Psychology, Kean University

Figure 8.2 Donald R. Marks
Photographer: Suzie Lee, The Photocoop

Donald R. Marks is Associate Professor and Director of Clinical Training for Kean University's Doctor of Psychology Program in Combined School and Clinical Psychology. A clinical health psychologist by training, Dr. Marks works with individuals and families facing chronic pain and illness as well as with athletes and performers recovering from injury. His current research also focuses on compassion-focused acceptance and commitment therapy for trauma-related conditions and on the social determinants of psychological distress. He is the editor, with Andrew Wolanin and Kendahl Shortway, of *The Routledge Handbook of Clinical Sport Psychology* (2021).

What's the role and importance of nurturing environments in the workplace?

Nurturing environments can make all the difference in a workplace. Current psychological science offers several ways to think about this. One place to start is the work of Peter Gray, author of *Free to Learn*. Gray argues that human beings primarily learn through play and that environments that invite opportunities for play also foster psychological well-being and encourage creativity. We can also think about work environments in behavioral terms. Nurturing or supportive environments make it possible for people to exercise the broadest behavioral repertoire, which is more likely to make innovation possible. Environments structured through authority and obedience foster consistency of a kind, but they quickly begin to rely on fear and intimidation, which narrows behavioral repertoires by emphasizing conformity and self-protection. Contextual behavioral science has examined the benefits of psychological flexibility in sustaining human well-being. Unsupportive environments tend to elicit less flexible behavioral responding, which makes it much more difficult for human beings to adapt to change. Psychologist Steven Hayes writes usefully about this in his recent book, *A Liberated Mind*. Also, as the evolution scientist David Sloan Wilson (*This View of Life*)—and many others—have noted, cooperative groups significantly outperform competitive groups. Nurturing environments foster cooperation and collaboration.

Why is it important for everyone to aim for diversity, equity, and inclusion?

The intensification of meritocratic striving for recognition and validation through economic success or social prestige has led us to recognize that the playing field is desperately unfair. The philosopher Michael J. Sandel writes compellingly about these issues in *The Tyranny of Merit*. As the saying goes, some people begin life on third base and think that they have hit a triple. At the same time, others aren't even allowed to set foot in the batter's box. Diversity, equity, and inclusion are vital to transforming the cruelty of this game and creating a more collaborative, nurturing human community.

The philosopher James Carse describes the difference between "finite games" and "infinite games." Finite games, he says, have a winner and a loser. A baseball game, a football match, these—at least to a significant extent—are finite games. Infinite games, by contrast, have a completely different focus. The aim of an infinite game is not to win but to keep the game going. Playing catch is an ideal example, as are those great children's games where everyone attempts to keep a balloon from touching the floor. The point of an infinite game is collaboration—accommodating one another and adapting together to spontaneous changes. Diversity, equity, and inclusion make sense for countless reasons—particularly when we think about fundamental human rights and fairness—yet they also make profound sense in terms of the sustainability of human endeavor. What we can do together in a collaboratively adaptive way—inclusively and fairly—will be far more sustainable than any high-stakes economic competition.

Why should clients and other business professionals build trust on their cross-disciplinary teams? Please tell us about why trust matters.

Trust and collaboration have much in common. Collaboration for collective achievement is much more likely within the frame of "we're all in this together" than under the auspices of "every man for himself." Oddly enough, though, even distrust involves a certain degree of both trust and collaboration. The Cold War, for example, involved an enormous amount of cooperation to maintain, each side trusting the other to play by "rules" concerning espionage and the proliferation of weapons. Mutually assured destruction may be mad, but it is also a form of collaboration that entails certain elements of trust.

In business, it is common to create climates of scarcity—there are only so many promotions, so many bonuses, and so on. The notion behind these schemes is typically that they will motivate better performance—and, to a certain extent, they do. Companies likely would cease to use them if they didn't work at all. The problem is that they also create conditions that elicit only a certain kind of performance, one that highlights individual competition or the competition between small groups. Collaboration will inevitably be a part of any success, but scarcity-based competitions such as these push cooperative effort into the margins. Volunteer organizations in which people come together to work in the service of a shared value are often far more influential than organizations that focus on individual recognition and reward. Trust increases in the context of shared values, which in turn yields increased flexibility and diversity of opinion. What do the people coming together to form a business venture value? What do they want their community to be about?

In the absence of shared values, a climate of interpersonal distrust is likely to ensue. When you suggest an idea, my first thought isn't "Will that take us where we want to go?" but rather "What's in this idea for you?" In multidisciplinary environments, these doubts can form fault lines between disciplinary affiliations so that members of a given discipline become territorial and on guard for stratagems designed to marginalize or eliminate their role. In a climate of trust, however, much greater emphasis can be placed on what we're doing together—and what we're doing it for. Each person's contribution, regardless of its disciplinary origins, has intrinsic value.

How can cross-disciplinary team members productively and diplomatically discuss creative solutions?

The United States Institute of Peace offers a framework for communication that I have found helpful in every setting in which I've worked—from psychiatric hospitals to locker rooms. I first encountered it in the work of Lisa Schirch and David Campt, who published a book that I highly recommend to everyone, especially people in leadership positions—*The Little Book of Dialogue for Difficult Subjects*. The framework draws crucial distinctions between "debate" and "dialogue." As the authors note, debate is conducted with winning in mind, even if that means discrediting the views of others. The aim of dialogue, by contrast, is understanding another's perspective. When one listens to another person in the context of debate, one does so to find holes or flaws in the counterargument. In dialogue one listens to understand how other people have arrived at their perspectives and beliefs. The stance of a debater is one of inflexibility—"I'll hold my ground no matter what you say"—while the stance of the person in dialogue is open to new possibilities. Distrust is the ground of debate, with each participant anticipating attacks and traps. Dialogue favors trust and collaboration as participants share their views and work toward shared understanding. Finally, in the context of debate, emotions are often used to intimidate so that the opponent will back down, whereas in dialogue emotions express passion so that one can convey the meaning and quality of experience. Dialogue consistently promotes collaborative and nurturing relationships, while debate tends to promote an insular culture of defensiveness.

Is there a reason some people resist atypical, daring, or new thinking?

Generally speaking, what we might call "resistance"—or efforts to avoid or control change—emerges from fear. Fear narrows behavioral repertoires as people rely on behaviors that maximize safety. Conventional thinking is likely to emerge from cultures that emphasize threat or create conditions of intimidation. Many people have been raised in family contexts in which differentiation—separating and individuating to become one's unique person—is constrained. As the great family-systems theorist Murray Bowen explained, families may attempt to control and contain anxiety, particularly in times of social or economic stress, through emphasizing loyalty and togetherness at the expense of individual development. These kinds of invisible loyalties can be replicated in the workplace, where we often call them "groupthink," to borrow the old social psychology term from Irving Janis. A nurturing and dialogical environment that supports diverse perspectives and welcomes alternative viewpoints is likely to yield more new ideas than one that is guided by conformity.

You've posited this point of view: "Human beings cannot not collaborate."
Please explain.

As the communications theorist Paul Watzlawick once noted, "Human
beings cannot not communicate." Everything we do relative to one
another has a communicative function. Even when people have no specific audience in mind, their behavior conveys messages that other people can receive and interpret. All human communication also involves
at least a degree of collaboration. We participate in vast networks of
meaning through relational framing—words, body sensations, ges-
tures, images all become linked in various ways through our participation in language systems. There are important language processes at
the heart of selfing, for instance, such as deictic framing (see Louise
McHugh and Ian Stewart's *The Self and Perspective-Taking*), through
which we differentiate and coordinate between I-you, here-there, and
now-then relational responses. These are social processes in which we
collaborate, improvising together to discover workable ways of selfing
and relating. The Jain monk and spiritual teacher, Satish Kumar, artic-
ulates this interdependence with the phrase "you are therefore I am."
Contextual behavioral science, through recent work on relational frame
theory, highlights that we are embedded in and emerge from these
intrinsically collaborative and dialogical interdependencies between
ourselves and others and the world.

If there is an evolutionary (and, at the very least, social) importance to coop-
eration, how about then to collaboration?

I would say that cooperation and collaboration are, more or less, the
same thing—working together or, more broadly, behaving together for
a purpose. Perhaps we might think of collaborating on a specific project
as a circumscribed form of cooperation, though I suspect that there is
no meaningful cooperation without the prospect of collaboration and
little effective collaboration without cooperation. As evolution science
suggests, there is little likelihood that human beings could have come
to inhabit the earth in such large numbers without massive collaboration. When one examines the human organism, it is clear that it is by no
means the most efficient (long gestational cycles, neoteny), the best
defended, the strongest, or the largest of species. Cooperation, as mul-
tilevel selection theory suggests, particularly through problem-solving
communication, appears to have been the primary method of human

proliferation. Also, without working together, it seems that it would be impossible to have any human institutions. The question for fostering human creativity, I would say, is not whether human beings will collaborate but *how* they will collaborate—on what relational terms, for what purpose, and with what level of flexibility.

Note

1   "George Lois's Goodman's Matzos Stunt," *The Real Mad Men and Women of Madison Avenue.* June 19, 2013. https://www.thirteen.org/programs/real-mad-men/real-mad-men-and-women-madison-avenue-george-loiss-goodmans-matzos-stunt.

Index

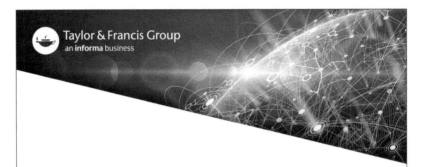